COLD WAR NAVY SEAL

COLD WAR NAVY SEAL

MY STORY OF CHE GUEVARA, WAR IN THE CONGO, AND THE COMMUNIST THREAT IN AFRICA

JAMES M. HAWES AND MARY ANN KOENIG

Skyhorse Publishing

10 9 8 7 6 5 4 3 2

Library of Congress Cataloging-in-Publication Data is available on file.

Cover design by Rain Saukas
Cover photo credit Lobert Broussard

ISBN: 978-1-5107-3418-0
Ebook ISBN: 978-1-5107-3419-7

Printed in the United States

Dedication

With much love and thanks to my children, Melissa, Liana, and James, and grandchildren, Jackson, Lily, Elizabeth, and William, for your love and for your forgiveness for all I should have done.

With deepest respect and admiration for the Congo Navy Cubans: loyal, brave, proud compadres. They put their hearts and guts in harm's way, not for fame, glory, or riches, but to contribute to the defeat of an evil philosophy; no medals, accolades, or even official recognition.

Rene Gough, "Gooch," the ultimate swim buddy (a special few will understand).

I hope this story, and the hostage rescue that triggered it, will help my children, grandchildren, and all readers appreciate:

(a) the contributions by special operations warriors and their families to the preservation of freedom and civilized behavior in your increasingly volatile and hostile world;

(b) the importance of intelligent, imaginative, and resolute leadership at all levels, and

(c) an appreciation for the diverse profiles of the men and women with the qualities of mental toughness, humanity, and courage to prevail at the tip of the spear on our country's behalf.

Contents

Acknowledgments • *ix*
Names and Places • *xi*
Preface • *xiii*
Introduction • *xv*

Chapter 1: Into the Heart of Darkness • *1*
Chapter 2: Incubating a Covert Warrior • *5*
Chapter 3: Vietnam • *13*
Chapter 4: Setting the Stage • *19*
Chapter 5: The Call • *29*
Chapter 6: Recruiting a Cutthroat • *41*
Chapter 7: Logistics Genius • *49*
Chapter 8: Covert Cuban Patriots • *63*
Chapter 9: Personal Differences • *69*
Chapter 10: Wrapped Around a Bottle • *81*
Chapter 11: Signs and Rumors of Che • *89*
Chapter 12: Threats from Every Direction • *95*
Chapter 13: Cuban Communists versus Cuban Americans • *103*
Chapter 14: Che Abandons the Fight. We Do Not. • *111*
Chapter 15: Corruption in the Congo • *123*
Chapter 16: Tragedy • *131*
Chapter 17: True Colors • *139*
Chapter 18: Mission Complete • *149*
Chapter 19: Post Script • *155*

Epilogue: A Reunion Fifty Years Later • *161*
Bibliography • *169*
Endnotes • *171*
Index • *175*

Acknowledgments

The events recorded in this book occurred over fifty years ago and are now declassified. The SEAL and CIA codes of secrecy have been honored over those years.

Any future historian will be forced to make assumptions and suppositions on the facts officially recorded in government archives, held in Washington, some 6,500 miles away from where these events took place. The circumstances will be examined by individuals with no firsthand knowledge of the events or the contexts in which they occurred.

This book attempts to accurately record the events by the remaining few who lived them, when and where they took place.

In appreciation of:
My Son: James, who may want to know me and my history better when he is old enough to be curious.
My Daughters: Melissa and Liana, who have urged me to write this since they were old enough to listen to my and my comrades' stories.
My Parents: "You can do anything, son. Believe in yourself."
My Brother: Mike, stalwart, faithful, always there.
Class 29 UDT/R (later BUD/S): life-long friends and Teammates with an unexplainable bond.
Wayland Academy/Ray Patterson: changed my life, maybe more than anything except UDT/R.
Mary Ann Koenig: cowriter of extraordinary patience, dedication, and determination; a real friend.
Rick Dobbis: constructive, wise advice.
Richard Leher: much appreciated and helpful legal assistance and expertise.
Howard Hart: one of fifty CIA "Trailblazers" and friend.

Robert "Pete" Peterson, USN SEAL ret.—Vietnam teammate, warrior, diplomat, gentleman

Manny Pichardo: faithful son of Ricardo Pichardo, dedicated to honoring and keeping alive the memory of the Cuban Congo Navy.

Brigade 2506 Museum and Library: for ensuring that the deeds and memories are not lost in the mists of time and to revisionist historians.

Alan Horn, faithful, unflinching friend

Larry Bailey, Tom Dunton, John Fleming, Tom Greer, Harry Humphries, David Janke, Mike Kammerer, Don Mann, Gage McAfee, Lou Morin, Roger Neff, John Roat, Bob Schoultz, Brad West, Maynard Weyers, Charles Hardeman, Janet Joy Ray, Per Bang-Jensen and others unnamed: all contributed.

Indonesia School of Business & Cultural Learning Institute: Original American Business Pioneers & Special Friends—like trying to explain SEAL bonds—What a book these stories would make: Dave Herron, Frank Morgan, Dan Emmett, Andy Bartlett, Joe Bartlett, Roger Perrin (token Scot), and those who have moved on too soon: Peter Jennings, Tony Granucci, Chase Waring.

Names and Places

The names of many cities and locations in Congo have changed over the years, principally after Joseph-Désiré Mobutu (Mobutu Sese Seko) came to power. Albertville became Kalemie, Léopoldville was changed to Kinshasa, and Stanleyville is now Kisangani. Elisabethville has become Lubumbashi.

I've changed the names of some of the people in this story for national security reasons, and in certain instances they were changed, as I saw it, simply to protect the guilty.

Preface

On a November morning in 1964, the skies over Stanleyville, Congo, filled with elite Belgian Régiment Para-Commandos, delivered into action by US Air Force C-130's. The joint operation, code-named "Dragon Rouge," remains the largest successful US hostage rescue mission in history.

The triggers for the operation were brutal massacres in and around Stanleyville in northern Congo, which became the catalyst for my mission. A Chinese- and Soviet-backed insurgent group, the Simbas, had captured Stanleyville the previous August and escalated their activities amid the political chaos raging throughout the Congo. They instituted a reign of terror that included torturing and killing missionaries and thousands of Congolese citizens while also taking hostage hundreds of white missionaries and US officials. They threatened to kill them all unless the US withdrew support for the current Congo government.

As the Belgians parachuted in to rescue the hostages and Lieutenant Colonel "Mad" Mike Hoare, the 5 Commando Commander and acclaimed British/South African mercenary, approached on the ground, the Simba rebels herded priests, nuns, and missionaries into Lumumba Square in downtown Stanleyville. Some attempted to escape and the rebels opened up and gunned down women and children in the streets.

During those horrible hours while the massacre began, a group of Cuban soldiers, led by an experienced American paramilitary officer, Rip Robertson, was operating independently with their own column. They began shielding children from Simba atrocities and shepherded many to the airport and out of the country. There were still many murders at the hands of the Simbas, but by the end of the day, Belgian paratroopers and US/Cuban-exile soldiers had expelled the rebels, rescued the hostages, and loaded hundreds of them onto US Air Force transport planes that flew them to safety.

One of the children was Ruth Reynard. Only four years old at the time, she was rescued by Juan Tamayo, a machine-gunner who sheltered her with one arm as he fired his weapon with the other during the five-mile ride from the missionary compound to safety. He covered her head to protect her from the expended, hot machine gun cartridges. For many years she believed that the man who saved her life was a mercenary. But she would learn later that he was a Cuban freedom fighter. "Imagine that," she said when she found out. "A Cuban in the Congo!"

Headlines around the world carried stories and photos of the horrific massacre and successful rescue. But none of the published accounts addressed what really happened.

In the urgent months that followed I was part of a team that built and launched the Force Navale Congolaise, a navy capable of defeating the rebels. Ultimately, we were instrumental in breaking the back of the Simba insurgency and my mission in the Congo would culminate in success. Along the way, we cracked an international political mystery. I was a twenty-six-year-old Navy SEAL, a Lieutenant (Junior Grade) posing as a much older Commander.

—James M. Hawes

Introduction

This is a firsthand, "names, dates, and places" account of what really happened inside a Cold War CIA program that's been kept out of the history books. It's the story of an American Navy SEAL who fought to aid a fledgling democracy in the Congo and stem the tide of communism in Africa. James M. Hawes built and commanded the Force Navale Congolaise, a clandestine mercenary navy at the very tip of the spear, and was point man for a successful, little-known paramilitary operation.

Hawes was commander of this covert Navy, a Vietnam vet of just twenty-six without a formal place in the chain of command. He frequently had to interpret situations, adapt, modify plans on the fly, and damp down confrontations among a group of brutal and self-serving mercenaries, all while delicately balancing between averting potential disasters and maintaining resolve. It's the story of an American naval officer under contract to the CIA who secretly built, staffed, and controlled a clandestine naval enterprise in a war zone in the heart of Africa. What they accomplished in the Congo is told in its entirety here for the first time, using recently declassified government documents, interviews with those involved, and most importantly, the memory of the commander himself.

* * *

At the time of the Stanleyville massacre, the Congo was only a few years into its declared independence from Belgium. And the country's mineral resources—the copper, cobalt, uranium, diamond, and gold deposits—had made it an attractive strategic battleground and a superpower pawn. Following independence, a secession war began in the mineral-rich Katanga Province. This rebellion unleashed other tribal insurrections that ravaged the Eastern Congo like a Cold War Ebola virus. Officials in the fledgling Congo government, and in the US, were preoccupied with combating communism, which they feared would lead to a loss of control over Congo's strategic mineral wealth and to diminished US influence throughout Africa. Chinese Premier Chou En Lai stated that the key to control of Africa is control of Congo.

Political strategy in the Congo had been muddled for the US. Throughout this period the policy had been to spread support to all political parties, covering all bets if one faction were to fall, so that ODYOKE (the cryptonym used to refer to the US government) would still maintain strength in its relationship with whoever was left standing. There was legitimacy to this strategy as local alliances were constantly shifting and a clear winner was not obvious. But the volatile Congolese government made that strategy a significant risk.

Congolese Prime Minister Tshombe and President Kasavubu displayed open hostility toward one another, which created concern in DC. The embassy and the State Department understood that any breach between the politicians would strengthen the rebel position and probably escalate the fight into an all-out national rebellion and civil war. "We are busting a gut to prevent a split between our two Congolese prima donnas—Tshombe and Kasavubu," a National Security staffer wrote to President Johnson.[1]

In Congo's capital city of Léopoldville, the CIA was getting nervous. The Agency's Chief of Station, Larry Devlin, sent a cable to Headquarters warning of the growing possibility of a loss of US influence in the Congo. Their concern at the time was about trust. ODYOKE had played all sides to win for so long in this volatile, unpredictable political climate that their reservoir of trust was "disturbingly low."[2]

Devlin continually urged General Joseph Mobutu, Commander in Chief of the Congolese forces, to help the two warring politicians get along and work together. But at one point Mobutu finally advised the COS that it was too late.[3] He believed that Kasavubu had already decided to remove Tshombe and appoint someone else. Fears of physical "liquidation"[4] spread through the Congolese government, and everyone was on edge.

Back in Washington, it was time for the US agencies to take matters into their own hands to maintain US influence in the Congo. While the anti-government rebel forces, the Simbas, were disorganized and volatile, the infighting in the Congolese government made the threat of their success real. Moreover, ODYOKE had good reason to believe the Simbas had monetary, if not personnel, support from Cuban and Soviet communists attempting to assert *their* influence. The US would need to take steps to weaken the rebel position and, in doing so, strengthen democracy and prevent the proliferation of communism in the region. And its discovery of US involvement was not an option.

All covert operations were administered by the 303 Committee, named after National Security Action Memorandum 303. The high-level, interdepartmental body, previously known as the Special Group, had been set up to approve and supervise covert operations. Because of the members' concerns about "speculative publicity" in recently published books concerning covert activity, the name was changed because it was believed that "303" reflected something "utterly drab and innocuous."[5] Peter Jessup, a member of the National Security Council staff, wrote in his May 1964 memo that all the suggested name changes were "repulsive but might suit our purposes."[6]

The 303 Committee (then as the Special Group) first approved major funding to strengthen a de facto government in the Congo on October 27, 1960. The job fell to the CIA. The Agency was aware that the Simbas were successfully transporting Soviet-supplied guns, ammunition, and supplies across Lake Tanganyika, nearly 450 miles long and 45 miles wide. On such a massive body of water, they had no problem remaining undetected, moving weapons and materials across the lake from dusk till dawn. From the declassified US documents, it's clear that the Congolese government was ringing alarm bells about how this unchecked weapons supply line was strengthening the rebels.[7]

Consequently, ODYOKE turned its focus to stopping the flow of guns streaming across the lake in support of the rebels, in order to help minimize the threat of Chinese or Soviet-bloc influence.[8] By the time of the Stanleyville Massacre, with the Soviet and Chinese-backed Simba rebels gaining strength, it was agreed to fund and put into action a "pocket Coast Guard," which would become the Force Navale Congolaise, the clandestine navy secretly built and commanded by James M. Hawes.

The Navy's mission was specific: stop the flow of weapons along Lake Tanganyika. But how to accomplish it would be left completely in the hands of a twenty-six year-year-old Lieutenant Junior Grade, fresh from running raids against the North Vietnamese.

—Mary Ann Koenig

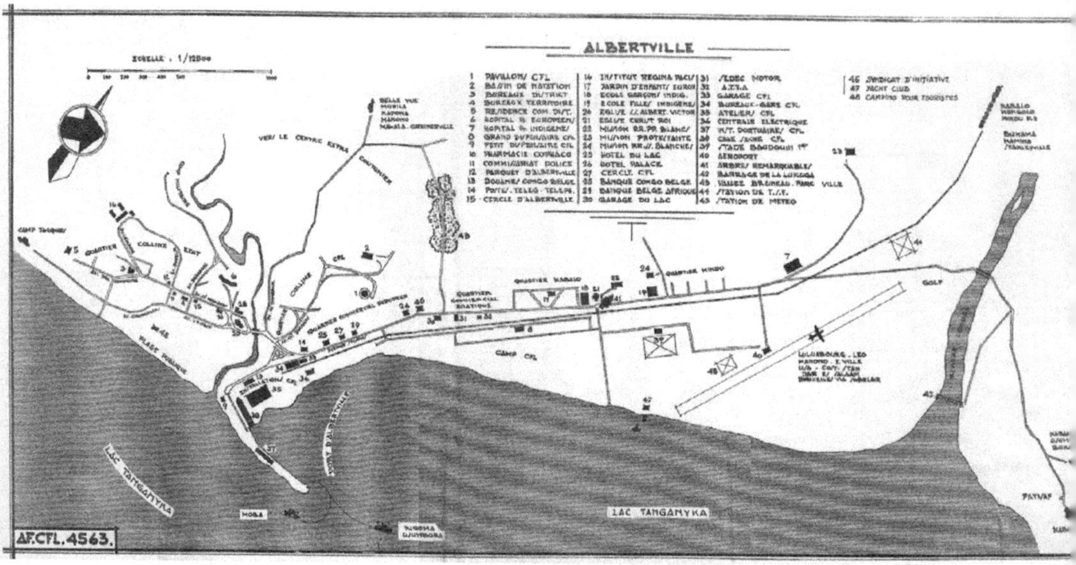

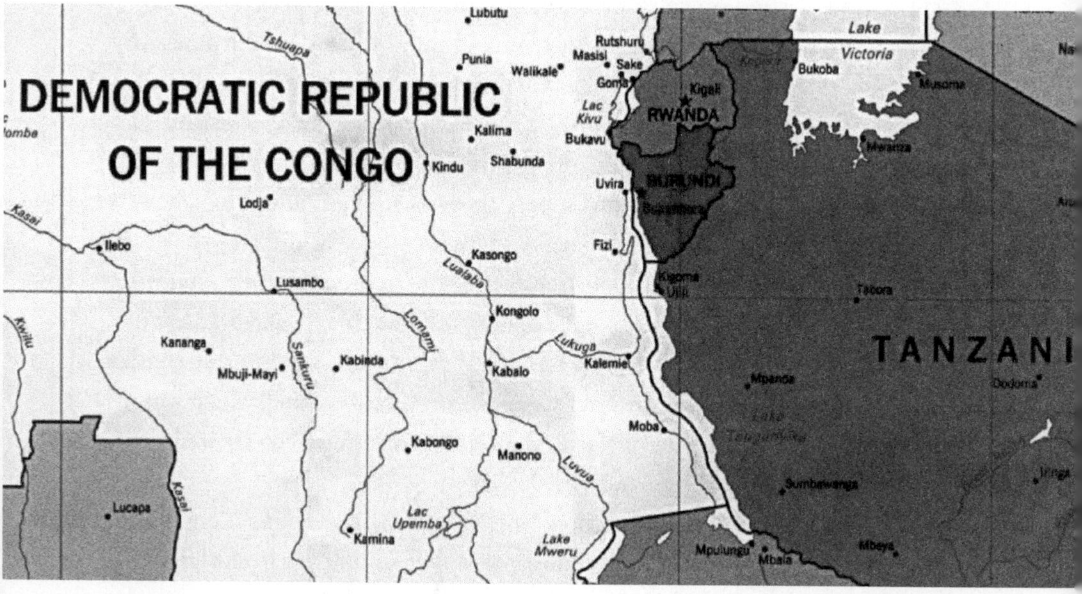

Note: Albertville changed its name to Kalemie as part of the Zairianization policies of the early 1970s.

Chapter One

Into the Heart of Darkness

Huddled on their knees on the floor of a dilapidated warehouse, a group of killers-for-hire glared up at me with that universal challenge: "Who the fuck are you and what are you doing here?"

I didn't know it at the time, but I was about to help them break into their safe.

A banging sound had brought me in here, blasting from behind the warehouse doors. It was a 1930s vintage structure perched across the midsection of a quay above the swampy overflow from Lake Tanganyika.

The clanging continued relentlessly even as I slid open the doors and stepped inside, coming face to face with this bunch of khaki-clad misfits. Weapons were either lying haphazardly on the floor or slung casually over their backs. Nearly every one of them had a sidearm strapped on. They were sullen and dirty, and a heavy cloud of black tobacco smoke soiled the air.

A dozen heads turned in my direction. They were pulled into a tight circle around a four-by-four metal safe, and one of them was beating the hell out of it with a crowbar. It was their spoils of war, the loot they'd "liberated" while on a recent assault. I had just crashed their party.

I knew these guys were 5 Commando mercenaries, LCol "Mad" Mike Hoare's troops. Probably the most famous mercenary in modern history, the colorful "Mad" Mike collected a hodgepodge of experienced soldiers, pretenders, and combat castoffs the way others collected stamps. He had ability and charisma, and never shied away from an opportunity to inflate his reputation. His exploits in Africa are said to be the inspiration for Daniel Carney's novel and film *The Wild Geese*, which starred Richard Burton and Roger Moore.

Over the next few months I would learn firsthand of the vicious nature of this 5 Commando band of cutthroats, the way they almost revered a code of duplicity instead of loyalty, and how their ruthless tactics adhered only to a pale version of military standard. These all-white paramilitaries from former British Colonies in Africa, Europe, and the UK were definitely not your well-disciplined combat troops. They had little respect for treatment of civilians and property, particularly safes, and they would demonstrate their shady conduct many times while I worked with them. But right now, I was having my maiden encounter, and it wasn't going that well.

My entrance was only a momentary distraction, however, and they quickly got back to work. The hellish banging started up again as one of them slammed the crowbar repeatedly across the safe. A tall, lanky guy in a dirty uniform walked up carrying a burlap sack. He fished a sizeable quantity of C3 plastic explosive out of the bag and began to pack it onto the safe. It was a pitiful sight.

I was a Navy SEAL, and the "D" in my UDT training stood for demolition, so I caught myself about to laugh at their amateurish blundering. This was my first indicator that professionalism was not the hallmark of a 5 Commando Congo mercenary. I was fresh from covert activities in Vietnam, well trained to improvise and survive, so I moved to a tactic that I hoped would give me the upper hand.

I knew that first impressions could make or break an officer and that this initial confrontation would be pivotal if I were going to succeed in the Congo. If the 5 Commando thought I had rank and knowledge on them, I would command their grudging respect. My mission was to build a mercenary navy and defeat the Communist-backed rebels, and 5 Commando would be the source from which I would recruit the naval personnel. Which meant I needed them to believe I had the US government behind me. Luckily for me none of them knew just how far behind. And if they made that assumption that I was a Commander, I wasn't going to discourage it. It was a good thing they didn't know I was just twenty-six years old, and only a Lieutenant JG. I stepped forward.

"What are you trying to accomplish?" I asked.

"We're getting into this safe," one of them responded with a decidedly irritated tone.

"Well, you're about to blow up the entire warehouse," I said. "And especially whatever's inside that safe."

They initially stared back at me with blank faces. These were twitchy guys, heavily armed, and the last thing I needed was to piss them off. Then I noticed that a few heads had begun to turn, and they were exchanging glances, looking around for reassurance whether they should believe me or not.

This was my opportunity. That edge of doubt was creeping in. I had knowledge they obviously didn't. I wasn't going to show them up, but I was going to show them the difference between real military training and make-believe.

"You want me to show you how to do that?" I asked.

There was no reply, just the physical gesture of them backing away from the safe, sullen and distrustful.

I was pretty sure that the mercenaries had heard that I had been sent there to remake everything. To build a navy, bring in personnel and boats, and run the operation. And I was aware that they were watching me closely. I knew that what I was doing at that moment would forge their impressions of me, and they would spread that word, for better or worse.

I leaned in and made an assessment of the safe, then picked up an empty tin can lying on the floor and formed a simple "shaped charge," an explosive technique used to focus the energy and the effect of the blast. I knelt over the safe and examined the mechanism, then I sectioned off just a small piece of C-3 and packed it firmly into the tin can. I positioned the can perfectly at the combination lock, properly inserted the blasting cap, and lit it up. There was a sharp blast and an intake of air from the anxious onlookers as a neat hole appeared where the lock had just been. I stood back and watched the door to the safe swing wide open.

The mercenaries mumbled their approval almost simultaneously as they dug for the contents. It was a paltry haul. An atmosphere of disappointment pervaded the warehouse as I turned to walk away and finish reconning the place for my new base of operations. There was a lot of work to be done to secure the old warehouse if I was going to run the mercenary navy out of there.

"Hey," one of the guys called after me. "Don't you want your cut?"

"No," I said. "It's yours."

I learned later that from this incident the word spread that the American should be well received.

But the American wasn't supposed to be there.

The Congo's recent independence from Belgium had triggered a secession crisis by one of the country's most mineral-rich and wealthy provinces. It led to an opening for the Soviet bloc to exploit rebellions among local tribal factions. The US saw the country as a strategic geopolitical necessity against communism, which meant the Congo was turning into a superpower battleground. The US feared that losing influence in the Congo was the next step to losing Africa.

The CIA had sent me to the Congo to conduct a clandestine operation, under as deep a cover as possible while still enabling and sustaining the conduct for a successful mission. The suits in Washington recognized that the communist rebels needed to be contained. The strategy was to cut off their supply lines and strangle their resource base, which would require battle-tested and seaworthy hands. And the world could not know we were responsible.

We were holding back the line on insurgent, violent communism. It was the boiling years of the Cold War and Africa was becoming a hotbed of potential dominoes that might fall the wrong way if we didn't pay attention. And as all eyes were focused on that other communist battleground in Southeast Asia, the US government wanted to keep Africa involvement as quiet as possible and ensure that no one could find our fingerprints on this op. Consequently, one of the most important elements in my Congo mission was to cover the ass of the US government. They needed a guy who had the knowledge and covert experience to make this a successfully play.

The CIA had determined that I was that guy.

Chapter Two

Incubating a Covert Warrior

My road to the Congo was a long one, and it started with my upbringing. I was lucky to be parented by a loving mother and father. They instilled in me the notion that I could do anything I set my mind to, which throughout my life has been both a blessing and a curse. They encouraged me to meet any challenge, make my own decisions, and live with the consequences. I grew up in Wisconsin and Texas and lived a small-town America life, with quintessential experiences like picking corn and peas for the local cannery in the summer, delivering newspapers on my bicycle on subzero Wisconsin winter mornings, and operating a jackhammer digging water wells during the blistering Texas summers. It taught me solid ethical values and an appreciation of hard work.

I was very fortunate to receive a scholarship to a wonderful school, Wayland Academy, in Beaver Dam, Wisconsin, for my entire high school period. Ray Patterson was the headmaster when I was there, and he went on to build two NBA teams, the Milwaukee Bucks and the Houston Rockets. He was a first-class mentor and changed my life. After my father, he was the man who influenced me the most.

After graduating from Southern Methodist University, I joined the Navy, like my father. He had been in the Pacific theater during WWII. Since childhood I had a dream of becoming a Frogman after seeing the Richard Widmark film *The Frogmen*. Years later I realized these circumstances of my upbringing had given me the character and spirit I would need to pass the rigorous Navy SEAL training.

After Officer Candidate School and being commissioned as an Ensign, I was ordered to the USS *Vega*, which was home ported in Oakland, California.

I completed Damage Control School and Atomic, Biological, and Chemical Warfare Defense School and reported aboard the USS *Vega* (AF-59) assigned as the Damage Control Assistant (DCA) and "R Division" (Repair Officer) in the Engineering Division. In one of life's ironies, I was the DCA and also the officer son of a WWII sailor. My father made every major sea battle in the Pacific from 1943 to the end of the war aboard the battleship USS *Maryland*. His battle station was in Damage Control. He was extremely proud of his son's commissioning, which is still a warm and vivid memory for me.

Toward the conclusion of my six-month cruise to the Western Pacific, the USS *Vega* was visiting the Yokosuka Naval Base in Japan and there I considered applying to become a Frogman. But my eyesight was enough to keep me out the SEALs altogether. To enter the Navy and attend Officer Candidate School to become an "unrestricted line officer," I needed a medical waiver. My eyesight was 20/200, the worst allowable under the required medical standards, if correctible to 20/20 with eyeglasses. So I purchased contact lenses with my first Navy paycheck. I was fully aware that my eyesight might prevent me from even entering the Frogman training.

I went to the Yokosuka Naval Base Hospital and timed my eye exam to occur during the lunch period. There was a corpsman striker, a medic-in-training, on duty in the ophthalmology unit. I knew his minimal medical experience would yield the least resistance to my desired result.

I said, "Corpsman, I need to get back to the ship. Can I read the chart to complete this exam?" With contact lenses in, I read the chart and passed with an excellent 20/15. There was nothing on any of the forms that questioned contact lenses or anything related, since the forms had not kept pace with technology. My application sailed through channels and I got immediate orders to report to Underwater Demolition Team Replacement Training, Class 29, commencing January 2, 1963. I was in.

Unlike enlisted personnel, officers carry their medical records between stations. I looked at my file, and saw the last page was the original waiver, the one that had allowed me to enter OCS with correctable vision. The waiver clearly showed my uncorrected eyesight as 20/200. It would have been so easy, right then, to remove that page containing the waiver. But I just could not do it. It would have betrayed my oath as an officer. In my mind, I saw a distinction between taking advantage of the fact that standard forms were not up to date with science and actively removing a document from my file.

Wearing my contact lenses, I'd already taken my pressure test in a decompression chamber, which took me down below 200 feet simulated water depth. I knew my contact lenses would enable me to do all that was required and that I would not endanger my teammates or myself.

Finally, I was off to the US Naval Amphibious Base, Little Creek, Virginia, with my original waiver regarding my eyesight safely and securely inside my medical file, praying that it would not be scrutinized.

Entering training was a whole different world. There were grueling, twelve- to fourteen-hour days of endurance events—swimming, running, climbing, and combinations. Or others that concentrated on demolitions or covert harbor and beach reconnaissance, night exercises paddling into the beach, hiding the rubber boats, patrolling to an objective, then withdrawing out to sea, undetected. But always water work—some days spending twelve or more hours in the water, interspersed with rigorous physical challenges. We'd run and swim seemingly endless miles, or navigate obstacle courses, and our boat training, always conducted in the heaviest surf available, went on continually, day and night, moving from one event to the next with a 250-pound rubber boat perched on the heads of our seven-man boat crew.

It was relentless action designed to allow you to learn that your physical limitations are imposed by your mind. But it wasn't just endurance or physical stamina and strength. There were other important lessons embedded there, such as the triumph of mental toughness and the appreciation of the concept of "team." Exhaustion causes mistakes, and at those moments mental fortitude needs to take over. "Strong of mind and body" wasn't just a catchphrase, it was a reality, with the emphasis being strong of mind, since many quitters were very strong of body.

One thing those training days made clear was that looks truly were only skin deep. Guys who seemed to have it all—tall, muscular, fast—sometimes fell out quickly. And others with little obvious physical ability persevered through a sheer strength of will. In those most extreme circumstances I saw men who would rather die than quit. We all had to be alert for it, particularly our instructors who were responsible for every trainee's safety. The last thing anyone wanted to see was a guy lying lifeless at the bottom of the pool or ocean. I remember an afternoon when that was exactly what happened.

We watched an officer swimming with forty-pound packs become so exhausted that he simply threw up his arms and sank rather than quit. Luckily for him there was an alert instructor there who saw this and fished him out. They quickly shot some air into the guy, then threw him back in the water. He finished the training.

There was another officer in my class who could not do the free dives to sixty feet because his ears would not clear. I remember his last chance. He went down and surfaced holding the stone, proof that he had done it, plus two broken eardrums—that is pain. He was kept out of the water for a couple of days for the eardrums to start to heal, then he was back at it.

It's no mystery to me that there is such mutual respect and camaraderie in SEAL training. It produces a belief that any challenge can be overcome, and that the most important value is the one of "team." Going through BUDS (Basic Underwater Demolition/SEAL training) allowed me to work with individuals who understand mutual support under any conditions. This intense training and the trust that develops are unique to the US Navy SEALs.

Halfway through training, Class 29 was down to the hardcore few; the quitters had been jettisoned away. Now, only an injury would drop a trainee out of the program.

But at formation one morning, my nightmare began. There had been a discovery of my original 20/200 waiver at the Bureau of Medicine and the 20/15 discrepancy in my eye exam allowing me to enter training, which the ophthalmologist called "a medical phenomenon." Over the next few days I was bounced from instructor to training officer to ophthalmologist. The instructors at the training unit had tested me by the most rudimentary standards—a hand held in the air and a demand of "Mr. Hawes, how many fingers do you see?" I had been told by the training officer that I might be eligible for a court martial, and the ophthalmologist had assured me that I was not a medical phenom, and that there was absolutely nothing to revoke the lethal "20/200" test result.

At every stop, I would recount the same truthful story to every officer, leaving out none of the details. Absolute truth was my only hope. My future as a Frogman was in serious jeopardy.

Finally, I reached the court of last resort—the Senior Medical Officer of the Atlantic Fleet, the Admiral. I had stood at attention in so many meetings, telling my story, that by the time I came before the Admiral I knew I had to take a calculated risk. I had reached the end of the line and had nothing left to lose. As he surveyed me with a pair of piercing eyes that looked as though they were examining my soul, I was unable to remain silent any longer. I took a breath and with all the intensity I could muster I said, "Sir, I am standing first in my class at this time, so don't tell me that I am not physically qualified."

He stared at me for another interminable period, the silence thick and gnawing. He knew what he was doing. He was waiting for me to cave. I stood rigidly and fiercely at attention. Finally he said, "All right, I will recommend a waiver."

It had never been done before. I thanked him and said that I would make him glad of his decision. I saluted and withdrew. Elated, I raced back to the training unit to face the punishment I knew awaited me. I'd been absent for far too long and my instructors were going to make sure I paid. And even that made me happy.

I will always be grateful for a Navy that produces officers who are not afraid to judge a situation on its merits. Maybe that is part of the culture of "command at sea," where there is no passing or spreading around responsibility, and the captain is entirely accountable. But I still didn't know if the waiver would be approved, and if I would be in training or out.

In those days, all training was conducted by the Naval Amphibious Schools command, not the operational UDT/SEAL Teams. And after a few days of uncertainty, I reported to the Commanding Officer of the Naval Amphibious Base, a "four-striper," Captain Lee, who told me he had on his desk a request for a waiver so that I could complete training. He said he could forward it approved or disapproved. Then he asked, "How would you like to come back as an instructor?"

I assured him enthusiastically that I would be very pleased to return as an instructor after I operated in the Teams for a couple of years. He responded in an even tone. "I don't think you understood me, Ensign. I have a waiver here for you to complete training that I can forward either approved or disapproved. How would you like to come back as an instructor?"

I got the captain's message loud and clear. "I would love to come back as an instructor, sir," I said.

I completed my basic training within six weeks, went to Army Airborne Jump School at Fort Benning, Georgia, and Underwater Swim School in Key West, Florida. Then I reported into the UDTR/BUDS training unit to be the boss of the very instructors who had been busting my butt. As true professionals, from my first day as Assistant Training Officer my fellow instructors treated me as if I were a renowned twenty-year veteran. It turned out to be the best working year of my life.

During the entire time I was an instructor and despite Captain Lee's coercion, I continued to try and get to an operational team, and I wanted that to happen sooner rather than later. The teams came under a separate chain of command and I knew they needed officers. I managed to get orders to report to the Teams, UDT-21. Then the phone rang. "Ensign, this is Captain Lee. You get your butt over to my office immediately."

As I stood at attention, he unloaded.

"You Frogs are always pulling crap like this. We have a deal. You are an instructor at the training unit and I will get these orders canceled right now." And he did. But the waiver to the operational teams was in place, and in effect.

Almost a year later I received a phone call from Tom Tarbox, SEAL Team 2's XO. He was calling with the kind of offer I'd been waiting for. "I have two questions," he said. "One—do you want to be assigned to Vietnam on a mission so secret that it comes straight out of (Defense Secretary) McNamara's office? And two—how soon can you be ready to go?" I replied "Yes, sir." And "Twenty-four hours."

There were very few officers available with my experience, and Tarbox knew I was more than ready to join an operating team.

When Captain Lee heard about it, he was infuriated with me all over again, thinking that I had circumvented him and the agreement we had made. He summoned me to his office yet again, and after venting his fury he picked up the phone to get my orders to Vietnam canceled.

I struggled to hold in the surging joy as I watched his demeanor turn from imperious to obedient. He finally hung up and said, "Congratulations,

LTJG Hawes. Whatever it is, it's so politically sensitive it comes straight from Secretary McNamara's office. Is there anything I can do to assist you?"

So I was off to Vietnam. I reported to SEAL Team 2 the next day and had a cup of coffee with Tarbox. And my life as a covert operator began.

After detaching from SEAL Team 2, bound for Vietnam, I stopped to visit my parents and brother. By that time, I was a trained and fit Frogman headed for war and the pursuit of my dreams.

As I concluded the visit with my folks, my mother put her arms around my neck and said, "Jim, take good care of yourself. Please tell them not to send your body home if you get killed. I could not go through it twice."

Her words were liberating to me. I knew it was hard for her to let me go, but also I understood, and always had, that she wouldn't try to deter me. Maybe you had to grow up as she did, in the heart of the Dust Bowl and as the wife of a WWII sailor on a battleship, to be able to be that strong.

It was typical of her to be encouraging of whatever I had wanted to do. Yet saying goodbye to me twice, once as I departed for war and then again as a casualty, wasn't something she would do. But there were no guilt trips, no whining, she didn't cry, she was completely supportive without a selfish gesture of any kind. Her only other request was, "just please write."

I was ordered immediately to the Military Assistance Command-Vietnam, Special Operations Group, Naval Advisory Detachment based in Da Nang, where I would spend the next year participating in the takeover of the CIA's Operation 34-A and its expansion and intensification under the Department of Defense.

Chapter Three

Vietnam

Through my DOD and CIA briefings, I had the initial impression that the CIA understood the nature and purpose of covert operations—small and limited in scope. We were told that Secretary McNamara viewed these activities during his 1964 tour and concluded that if these small and limited covert operations were effective, then they'd work even better when enlarged and expanded. How the operations would remain anywhere close to covert and limited was apparently ignored or dismissed.

In early '64, MACV-SOG (Military Assistance Command Vietnam—Special Operations Group, formerly Studies and Observations Group) was created. Under this authority and McNamara's direction, the military would take over OP PLAN 34-A where a principle strategy included the establishment of the Naval Advisory Detachment, employing small boats to run harassing raids against North Vietnamese installations. All 34-A maritime operations were approved by President Johnson's National Security Advisor McGeorge Bundy and communicated directly to NAD, Da Nang, with a copy to inform Saigon. Targeting was done in the vault at Bach Dang, where the intel was secured and ops planning took place, including proficient aerial photography (pre-satellite imagery) interpretation by a Navy Intel Lieutenant who was an essential part of that mix. The SEALs took part in planning the operations and conducted the training of the raiding teams, which were made up of South Vietnamese Navy personnel. I was assigned as Training Officer and Assistant Operations Officer to help run the operation.

On arrival in Da Nang we moved into Bach Dang, the building previously occupied by the CIA. Soon after, a Marine Major assigned as the operations officer joined us. Jim Munson was intelligent, open-minded, and professional, and an excellent role model. China Beach was our training area, off-limits to all other military or civilians. For our purposes, the CIA had built six camps, one every mile for six miles along the beach. The teams were rigidly compartmented from any contact, so that there could be minimal possibilities of betrayal in the event of capture. Years later that beach became an in-country R and R location, as well as the setting for the TV series *China Beach*.

Since there were no precedents, no manuals or procedures for what we were doing, the learning curve was dramatic and we were only limited by imagination and what we could make work. There was no way of knowing or anticipating how applicable these lessons would be in the future.

Our group was a plausibly deniable, clandestine operation and needed to stay that way. We had to avoid not only our own media, but also the International Control Commission (ICC), a group of three inspectors representing Canada, Poland, and India who were tasked with monitoring aggression in the region. An important part of my mission was to avoid the ICC, because the North Vietnamese were protesting our raids and trying to bring international public attention to our actions, while Secretary of State Dean Rusk repeatedly and publicly denied our existence.

We utilized disguised fishing boats (junks) and aluminum fifty-foot "Swifts," CIA assets already in place that were extremely reliable and capable of speeds up to twenty-five knots. They were subsequently supplemented by Norwegian "Nasty-Class" PT boats, which we called Nasties. They were ninety-five feet long, laminated plywood with high-performance Napier-Deltic diesel engines capable of making forty-five knots. We began using the Nasties almost exclusively, because they could outgun and outrun anything the North Vietnamese had on the water at the time. They could deliver and recover teams quickly, and after the bombing in the north commenced, these boats could harass North Vietnamese radar sites utilizing the 40mm guns and subsequently 81mm mortars, which we installed later.

I trained the boat crews and over-the-beach assault teams to run clandestine sabotage and psychological raids above the seventeenth parallel—into North Vietnam. It was hit-and-run warfare.

We ran night operations on the water for several months, staging amphibious raids or mortar bombardment on radar installations, striking deep into the heart of enemy waters. Those raids had a direct, historical, and psychological impact and played a critical role in the most significant catalyst for escalation of US involvement and a full military commitment to the war: the Gulf of Tonkin incident.[9]

On the night of August 3, 1964, we were ordered up the coast under cover of darkness to hit extremely sensitive North Vietnamese radar installations and security bases at the islands of Hon Niu and Hon Mat.

We sent the Nasties up there, knowing they'd get the job done quickly. These islands are in the direct path to the entrance to Haiphong Harbor and hitting them could have been considered a threat to Haiphong itself. We came in fast and hit the targets hard and successfully. When we finished, the North Vietnamese patrol craft came after us with a fury, chasing us back down toward Da Nang. Our boats outran them somewhere north of the seventeenth parallel.

Those North Vietnamese Swatows that were chasing us that night were the ones that allegedly attacked the USS *Maddox* and the USS *Turner Joy*. And our attacks on them most likely triggered their strategy to engage the US in retaliation. What happened with us and the *Turner Joy* and *Maddox* on that night would result in the joint Congressional Tonkin Gulf Resolution, which authorized President Johnson to escalate US military efforts in Vietnam.

We berthed the Nasties at the NAD Base at the foot of Monkey Mountain near the entrance to the bay in Da Nang. And then we heard from Saigon. Because of the possibility of an immediate response by the North Vietnamese following their failed "attack" on the US destroyers, Headquarters was concerned that we and the Nasties should seek immediate shelter further south at Cam Ranh Bay.

I was the sole American, and officer-in-charge, as the Nasties departed Da Nang. Our only knowledge of what awaited us at Cam Ranh Bay was a vintage 1903 French chart. We stocked the boats with sacks of rice and jars of *nuoc cham*, a pervasive Vietnamese chili and sweet seasoning, and a satchel full of piasters to cover necessities. We had no idea of the conditions on the scene or the length of time we might be there. We also had the additional challenges of obtaining fuel for the boats while ducking the ICC inspectors.

Since the Nasties were the potential target, the Swifts remained in Da Nang. When we arrived at Cam Ranh Bay we were welcomed by the South

Vietnamese Navy Junk Force "Dai Wei" (Captain), along with SEAL LTJG Bob "Pete" Peterson, dispatched by SOG/Saigon to provide judgment and support. Pete is what the SEALs call a "Plank Owner," one of the original members of the first SEAL teams created by President Kennedy and activated January 1, 1962, ST-1 (West Coast-based) and ST-2 (East Coast-based), respectively. Pete and I would work closely together in Vietnam and were among the first SEALs from ST-2 to have PCS status (permanent change of station) early on in the war. He would become a lifelong friend.

I was one of five officers who made up NAD's start-up core group in Da Nang. There was another SEAL, LCDR Ken Wolfe, from CO UDT-21, a civil engineering corps officer, an administrative officer. And there was the officer-in-charge, J. D. Bowens, a destroyer officer with no special operations training or experience.

Younger SEALs cannot appreciate the atmosphere in those days. The Frogmen and early SEALs were barely tolerated by the traditional Navy, and 34-A was the most politically sensitive operation in the country. Ignorance and disinterest in covert operations, along with security compartmentalization, made it inevitable that the Navy would appoint an officer-in-charge with no training, no experience, and no interest in a vessel smaller than a destroyer.

The miscasting of Commander Bowens can best be summarized by a remark he made in the bar of the Majestic Hotel in Saigon. We received three-plus days of briefings that included numerous references to Ho Chi Minh: Ho this; Uncle Ho that; Ho Chi Minh here and everywhere. Repeatedly. At the close of each day we would gather for a beer and a wrap-up in some "get-better-acquainted" sessions. Every evening Commander Bowens would gripe about being in Vietnam rather than on his destroyer home ported in San Francisco.

Prior to our departure for operational headquarters in Da Nang, and after three full days of references to Ho Chi Minh, Commander Bowens, in charge of the most politically sensitive operation in Vietnam, leaned over his beer and growled, "Say, just who in the hell is this Ho Chi whatever-his-name-is, anyway?"

Bowens was not good with or considerate of subordinates. I felt as though a VC plant in the Bureau of Personnel had assigned Commander Bowens to this post. He moved into a beautiful villa, and when cement was difficult to obtain and needed over at the training area to build facilities, it usually went to the construction work going on at his villa.

I have tried to think of something positive to say about him, but unfortunately, it's not possible. He guarded his authority and position jealously, was not a team player, and also was not very smart.

He thought the SEALs were lower forms of Navy personnel because they did not serve on ships. I think Maynard Weyers, a prominent, respected career SEAL Officer, OIC of the ST-1 detachment for six of those twelve months, would agree on this point: a big part of my job was to insulate the SEALs, who conducted the training of the raiding teams, from Commander Bowens. But dealing with him was part of what I had to go through in Vietnam in order to be prepared for the Congo. There I learned the clandestine art of plausible deniability and gathered the experience that led me to build and lead a mercenary navy for the CIA.

I was incredibly lucky. I was being paid to do what I would have done for free.

Chapter Four

Setting the Stage

While I was learning covert ops on the job in Vietnam, the Cold War was heating up in Africa. What preceded my arrival in the Congo was an extraordinary effort that included the talents of an American operator, Jordy McKay. He did everything he was supposed to do, and more.

As a one-man show, McKay was in the Congo to work with 5 Commando and he made up the entirety of the US clandestine, maritime, paramilitary team. The Agency had sent him there before they sent me, and no contribution was more vital to mission success than McKay's. But through an event in the middle of a crucial battle, McKay made a judgment and acted on it—and it was exactly the wrong decision, according to the State Department. Because of that, the operation became available to me. But the groundwork for our mission success lay in the actions McKay took at a place called Fizi Baraka.

* * *

At the beginning of 1965, the US actually thought the Congo's turmoil seemed to settle. National Security Advisor Robert W. Komer wrote that he saw a "bit of blue sky in the Congo."[10] But he warned that a rebel counteroffensive would mean a setback, and that's exactly what happened. By late February, the situation was again hot. President Johnson received a memo from the NSA saying, "the rebel counter-offensive we've feared may have begun."[11]

This Congo battlefield had heated and cooled to a varying degree of ferocity over the preceding several years. The Simba Rebels were a ragtag bunch of untrained renegades more interested in pillaging and butchery than ideology or cause. But then they began to receive the support of communist advisors and troops, who had been training in Eastern Europe and China, and supplies of weapons and ammunition steadily increased. The US worried that with Soviet-bloc training and reinforcements, the Simbas might actually turn into a coordinated fighting force. That notion began to drive policy.

That was part of the reason McKay was sent there. He was a graduate of the US Merchant Marine Academy and a former Navy Explosive Ordnance Disposal officer. He had four years of Agency experience conducting maritime and paramilitary operations against Castro's Cuba. He knew the tactics, understood the strength of the fighting force, and spoke fluent Spanish.

In the mid-1950s, McKay left the Navy to start a salvage business in Cuba. In the years just after the revolution, when commerce still existed between the US and Cuba, he continued to run his business from Havana.

But as with all fledgling dictatorships, Castro needed a patron. As his regime turned more east than west, and the USSR saw the strategic advantage of controlling a puppet state just ninety miles off the US mainland, the environment in the country began to change. McKay soon found his business prospects curtailed by a paranoid Castro government.

On a tropical Havana afternoon, Cuba's Minister of Industry summoned McKay to his office in the government palace just off the Malecón overlooking Havana Harbor. The atmosphere of intimidation couldn't have been more apparent. The minister demanded to know why McKay was importing equipment from the USA and not the USSR. From that meeting on, things went downhill for his business in Cuba. Customers stopped coming around. Inventory disappeared and he found that no one was willing to work with him. Eventually, after frustrating months of government intrusion, he was forced to leave Cuba.

The Cuban Minister of Industry who pressured McKay out of business was Che Guevara. Five years later, on a remote peninsula halfway around the world on Lake Tanganyika in the Congo, McKay would collect some of his payback.

McKay retuned to the CIA after Guevara forced him out of Cuba. Bill Hamilton and Tom Clines assigned him to Albertville, just as Hamilton would recruit me to the job after McKay left. Hamilton, the chief of the CIA's Maritime Branch of the Special Operations Group, was the former Frogman

Commander and a Naval Academy graduate. The son of an admiral, he had stellar career accomplishments, including being in the Pentagon at the right place and time to influence the Department of Defense's ideas in forming the SEALs.

Hamilton was a large, imposing fellow and in addition to being a Frogman was a carrier-landing qualified Naval aviator and a Korean War veteran. He was the kind of guy who made it easy for people to cooperate with him. I saw him work that charm many times but never quite got his talent to rub off on me.

Tom Clines was his deputy and together they made a formidable combination. A highly decorated Korean War vet with five bronze stars, Clines was a well-traveled, imaginative, very experienced CIA case officer who had been involved in the Agency plans to overthrow Fidel Castro. Together they hatched the Congo Navy operation plan and came up with an ingenious scheme.

The maritime interdiction operations McKay was running would be a prelude to my assignment to establish the Force Navale Congolaise. There was sketchy intelligence percolating from the area that indicated that the Chinese were heavily involved and the US wanted to prevent Communist China (PRC) from freely transporting weapons up the lake to the pro-communist Simba Rebels operating in the northeast.

Rebel supply lines were complicated. Weapons had to be brought by ship from China to the Tanzanian port of Dar es Salaam. Then they were trucked overland nearly 500 miles through Tanzania to the Congolese lake port of Kigoma. Finally, after a months-long journey, they would be loaded onto a variety of lake vessels and would then sail hundreds of miles up Lake Tanganyika, arriving in enemy enclaves along the lake's eastern shores.

Fizi Baraka, the quasi-headquarters for this sloppy but lethal group, lay on the northwestern part of Lake Tanganyika near the border of the provinces of Northern Katanga and South Kivu. It became McKay's target; the battle would mark the beginning of the end for the Simbas, or so it was thought. It was supposed to cripple the rebel movement by engaging and defeating their main force.

But that was a very loose interpretation of the uniformity of the rebels' structure. The rebel command was an equal opportunity, dysfunctional group.

Numerous factions played off one another at the whim of the individuals' leaders and tribal loyalties. Disorganization nearly put them out of business altogether except as traditional bandit groups, raping and pillaging with no political motivations or objectives. As the mission proceeded and I arrived, it would become clear that eliminating one group would not necessarily have a bearing on others.

But on that summer night, McKay and LCol "Mad" Mike Hoare's 5 Commando mercenaries were about to bring the fight to the rebels' doorstep. They would do it in spectacular fashion.

McKay and Hoare were using the *Ermans*, a 120-foot cargo ship that I would co-opt and utilize when I incorporated her into the new fleet of the Force Navale Congolaise a few months later. The *Ermans* had been converted into a gunship and armed with .50 cal machine guns later augmented by Russian 12.7mm machine guns. She also had a formidable 75mm recoilless rifle at the stern. McKay had successfully lobbied for and succeeded in adding radar to the ship, which would prove immediately useful in the pitch-black nights on the lake.

5 Commando would travel with a small armada of vessels and barges 150 miles up Lake Tanganyika from Albertville. They'd make an assault from the lake, cross the beach to the rebel's main stronghold, and then advance overland and clear the road to Fizi. Hoare's plan would contain the enemy in a semicircle, at the center of which was Jungo, a port town that held rebel-training headquarters.

They acquired an imposing lake steamer, the *Urundi*, from a Belgium-owned maritime company. Since this company was barely still operating in the Congo, it showed enthusiastic support for the enterprise in hopes that their intra-lake commerce could be resurrected. They prepared *Urundi* to carry troops and to tow several heavy barges loaded with vehicles, weapons, and equipment. Belgian engineers lent their expertise and McKay designed special ramps to attach to each barge. They could then off-load a number of vehicles onto the beach, including four five-ton trucks, four jeeps, and four light armored cars manufactured by the British auto company Daimler. The "Ferrets," as they're known, weighed about three tons each and were outfitted with two types of machine guns. Sporting Rolls-Royce engines, the Ferrets were fast, topping out at a speed of about 50 mph.

All told, the invasion fleet would employ approximately one-third the total number of troops used in the Bay of Pigs. A small covey of vehicles, plus nearly 300 mercenaries, would land ashore that day.

The *Ermans* and the fleet of Seacraft-21s were manned by Hoare's troops of Brits and white Africans from South Africa, Zambia, Kenya, and Rhodesia—all of them from 5 Commando, but none of them actual experienced naval personnel. McKay had this woefully inadequate talent pool to work with, but because of his background, he was able to execute the plans and train the boat crews for this specific assault.

On the night of the attack as the convoy of boats motored toward the target on the ink-black water of Lake Tanganyika, a powerful storm came out of nowhere. Unexpected heavy seas mired the mission with rolling waves crashing over the bow and lightning strikes firing up the darkness. The slog across the lake under those conditions put the operation nearly two hours behind schedule.

Hoare's book *Congo Mercenary* reports that his men were "blacked up" with burnt cork on their faces, ready to wade in and take the beach, but because of the storm and the threatening seas, the assault on Fizi Baraka nearly ended before it began.

When the landing force departed Albertville that night, Hoare believed Simba scouts might have spotted them, alerting the rebels that the invasion was underway. The Simbas could roam freely and undetected throughout Albertville, so McKay and Hoare suspected there was a high probability that their mission had been compromised.

At 0200, just before H-Hour, tropical lightning shattered the sky and lit up the flotilla in flashes as stark as daylight. LCol Hoare was convinced that the enemy had seen them and he called a unit commander's meeting aboard his flagship, the *Urundi*. There he announced that he was aborting the mission.

McKay protested immediately. He was certain they could still be effective even if the enemy suspected their arrival. After a tense back and forth, McKay convinced Hoare that the enemy had no specific information on intention and definitely couldn't know their landing spot, which meant they still held the element of surprise. Then, he was able to make his most important case: that an operation of this scope and complexity could not be remounted in the near future. Reluctantly, Hoare agreed to proceed.

During the assault McKay would make a significant difference in the war, albeit by making a conscious decision that would contravene CIA instructions. He wasn't supposed to be in the fight. The State Department wanted no US fingerprints on the operation, and plausible deniability was the purpose behind using 5 Commando boat crews. If a mercenary were killed in the Congo, so be it. But if an American turned up shot and dead there, particularly ex-Navy personnel, it would be much more difficult to ignore and whitewash away.

McKay was the only American officer involved in the planning, training, and preparation of this operation and, despite CIA instructions, ultimately the only one who unexpectedly ended up engaged in combat.

As dawn broke the first boats landed. In his book, Hoare tells of a "beach party" paddling a small assault boat through large waves, each successive one lifting the boat to a crest and then dropping it into a trough. Some of the men were violently seasick, vomiting between each stroke of the paddle.

As the troops and equipment started to arrive on shore and the assault began in earnest, McKay was shocked to discover Robert Rogers, an NBC News reporter, and his cameraman aboard the *Urundi* as invited guests of LCol Hoare. Rogers, an impressively well-traveled war journalist and award-winning documentary writer and producer, made some of the network's most important documentaries in the 1960s and '70s.

If the embassy had known that Hoare had press along for the raid that night, they definitely would have disapproved and even scuttled the assault. But Hoare never allowed a self-aggrandizing publicity opportunity to pass him by. The reporters were treated to a front-row seat as the operation got underway, but only in return for their assurance that they would not expose all the personnel involved. To their everlasting credit, Rogers and his colleague did not betray McKay's presence and critical contribution. They reported the events and honored the deal by resisting the opportunity for an exposé of the American.

The troops surged onto the beach, coming twelve at a time, emerging from the Seacraft-21s with McKay on the *Ermans* commanding all aspects of the amphibious phase. The barges came into shore and homemade ramps deployed perfectly, settling into shallow water and allowing the vehicles to make a relatively dry landing.

The enemy was taken by surprise by the speed and force of the attack, and Hoare and his troops soon established a significant beachhead. But then the snap of small arms fire could be heard in the distance, and heavy fire came ranging from deeper inside the brush.

Hoare tried to take his men forward and off the beach but enemy reinforcements appeared. Amid an increasing barrage of heavy fire, the rebel resistance stiffened and they mounted a surprisingly strong defense with accurate use of weapons. As 5 Commando forces took casualties, they became bogged down. Around H-Hour+3, the attack started to stall.

By this time the landed troops were critically short on ammunition. Hoare was dug in and tried to radio for fire support. From their position on the beach, the 5 Commando troops saw a small church on the left flank of the landing zone. Shrouded in vines and scrubs with a peaked wooden steeple, it soon became obvious that a well-trained pair of gunners was shooting from that steeple. With an unobstructed view of the beach, the snipers kept Hoare and his men pinned down by accurate fire.

McKay went to the captain of the *Ermans*, a 5 Commando mercenary under Hoare's command, and asked him to bring the boat around and to also get someone on the 75mm recoilless perched on the stern. But there was no response. McKay, face to face and under fire in the middle of battle, stared at a frozen captain who had gone gun-shy.

Without hesitation McKay took control of the ship himself. He ordered the helmsman to steer the *Ermans* parallel to the beach until they were approximately 150 meters off shore and only 250 meters from the machine gun nest. McKay called for a dead-slow course with the engines stopped and the *Ermans* began taking direct enemy fire. McKay ran to the aft deck and got on the giant 75mm weapon.

He had bore-sighted and tested the rifle the day before so he could fire with accuracy. He loaded the recoilless, took aim, and fired the powerful weapon at the steeple where the hidden gunners continued to pin down the landing troops. His first shot was a bullseye. The heavy rounds of the recoilless struck the machine gun nest with a force that demolished the steeple. Two bodies were flung into the air like a pair of rag dolls as the nest was splintered and blown apart. The gunners were silenced.

An eerie calm descended on the beach as the harassing machine guns stopped. Almost immediately the rebels began to retreat and gunfire faded slowly as they ducked away. But that would not be the end of the Simba Rebels. They would regroup and live to fight another day.

LCol Hoare began to plan a breakout that would take troops into the interior from Fizi to pursue the retreating Simbas. He buried his five KIAs. The enemy count was 215.

Soon after the assault when McKay was back in Albertville, he received an immediate message from Headquarters via Léopoldville. The news was shattering. His father had suffered a fatal heart attack. The NYPD detective had been on the job when he'd collapsed.

In Léopoldville, Chief of Station Larry Devlin arranged immediate transportation for McKay to return home to his family in time for the funeral. Jordy McKay never went back to the Congo.

McKay's employers viewed his action in the Fizi Baraka assault with conflicting attitudes. He had breached what today would be called "the rules of engagement." The embassy was outraged that he'd actually participated in the battle and had chosen to ignore the potential consequences if the operation had failed. The Africa Division wanted to fire him to appease the State Department. But the Special Operations Division (SOD) wanted to present him with the Intelligence Medal. They understood that McKay's intervention had saved the success of the operation. Unquestionably, the assault would have failed without his initiative. The two parties, with their widely conflicting opinions, never came to a resolution. But McKay had more than earned the respect of his peers and went on to a very successful career.

Once back in the States, McKay volunteered to his superiors numerous times that he was ready to return to the Congo, but he wasn't allowed to go back. That's when I was contacted and recruited, and I jumped at the opportunity to go to the Congo and establish a full-fledged Force Navale Congolaise, with its own naval personnel that I could select. It would be a force that would operate independently of 5 Commando.

McKay's courage under fire and clear-headed action in a critical battle at

Fizi Baraka had undisputedly saved the operation from calamity. But it would be a while before he found out who he'd been up against that day. Later, when I arrived in Congo and the Force Navale Congolaise came together, the Cuban-exile sailors who made up our team would do some clever detective work, and our Congo Navy would solve an intelligence mystery.

At Fizi Baraka, McKay got his payback. The Minister of Industry who had put him out of business in Cuba had been leading the rebel troops on the other side. It was Che Guevara. He'd been missing from the public scene for months, and there was nothing but international speculation as to his actual whereabouts. We found him in the Congo, trying to motivate and politically indoctrinate the disorganized Simbas.

When McKay pounded away on the 75mm recoilless rifle, he not only earned a personal victory, he also helped lay the groundwork so that a few months later our Force Navale Congolaise finally had Che on the run.

Chapter Five

The Call

My original assignment in Vietnam required that I volunteer to extend my service obligation so that I would have a full year tour in Vietnam. Toward the end of that year, I volunteered to the SEAL detailer at the Bureau of Personnel (BuPers) to extend a second time so I could take the first detachment of SEALs to the Mekong Delta. Since I would have a year's experience in country and because there were so few officers, BuPers was very pleased.

I knew the Delta would be a completely different operating environment and I asked BuPers to allow me to complete a proper training cycle back in Virginia Beach with my component of other SEALs, which would require that I leave Vietnam a month short of a year. BuPers said that couldn't be done because no personnel were ready to replace me on my current mission. So I acquiesced and accepted only a partial training cycle.

Eventually, I was relieved by two officers, both senior to me in rank. One was a classmate, Curt Gibby. When Gibby arrived, I commented on how it would have been helpful if he could have arrived a few weeks sooner so that I could have completed a full training cycle. He was surprised. "I could have done that, easily," he said. He'd just been biding time back home waiting until my original relief date.

I was on duty at that moment and I remember I was furious. Why couldn't BuPers have made that happen? Seemed to me there wasn't the slightest attempt to support my legitimate operational request, which was in the best interest of our mission, not just me.

What I considered cavalier behavior by BuPers drove me to the phone. I got through to Saigon, and then to Honolulu, and pretty quickly directly to the BuPers detailer's desk back in Washington, DC.

I gave him my name, file number, and then I made a critical demand. "I am on a voluntary extension," I told him. "And I want out of the Navy immediately." My indignation at what I believed was just laziness had got the best of me and I admit I didn't think it through. But the orders were forthcoming and I detached the next week to San Francisco for processing out of the Navy.

After separation, the tug of the Teams and my desire to return to the SEALs was irresistible. I made my way to Little Creek, knowing that I would sign up again so I could be right back in Vietnam and the Delta.

There are times in life when a wrong decision ultimately leads to a right circumstance. This turned out to be one of those. While back in Little Creek, I got a call from Phil Gattis, a SEAL Team 1 Plank Owner who had actually been embedded with the CIA in Da Nang during my tour. He was a terrific officer and we had worked closely together. We were the only two SEAL officers with significant Swift Boat experience.

I knew Phil was about to enter the CIA career training program, and I also knew that his wife was about to deliver their first child. He'd been tapped for the urgent, unanticipated Congo assignment at the same exact time that he was to start the career training program. Turning down the Congo would have been a very difficult decision for him, but it would be easier if he could recommend to the Agency another qualified candidate. In that initial phone call, his question was, "Are you interested?" My reply: "Absolutely. Does that mean I'll get paid, too?"

A few days later I received another call. That one from Bill Hamilton, Chief of Maritime Ops Branch of the Special Operations Division. My recruitment for the Congo interdiction navy was underway.

I met with Hamilton several times as he vetted me on the necessary skills and experience for the assignment. He then sent me to his boss, the SOD Chief, Bruce Cheever, a retired Marine Colonel with a major intellect and an abundance of experience.

The meeting was shorter than I had anticipated, undoubtedly a reflection of the trust Cheever had in Hamilton. It was clear that Cheever wasn't interested in my tactical qualifications; Hamilton had already vetted me on knowledge and experience and recommended me for the job. Cheever was supposed to evaluate my character and to determine whether this young man was going to execute the assignment or buckle under the pressure. I apparently met his standards.

With my Congo assignment assured, I quickly learned firsthand that working for the CIA was going to be a very different enterprise than being in the military.

At some point in the preparation for the mission, Col Cheever decided I needed to go through what the CIA termed an "OpsFam course," an operations familiarization course. It turned out to be a wise decision.

They presented me with a plane ticket to Tucson, Arizona. They told me someone would meet me at the airport and then take me to a base, which was a cover facility for people and aircraft used in CIA operations around the world. This ground facility would appear to be a legitimate, private aviation enterprise.

The CIA had taken over Marana Air Park, today known as Pinal Air Park, as Vietnam heated up, and the cover was a base of freight and maintenance operations. It was a principal base for Air America and Continental Air Services, the CIA's Southeast Asia operation. Over the years it has been used to train Air National Guard, and the US Forest Service has instructed its aerial firefighting crews there.

No one told me the name of the facility nor where it was located; all I knew was that I'd be landing in Tucson and be picked up there. But it was at Marana that I would get my general indoctrination.

I didn't know the name "Marana," nor anything about the "proprietary," which is a CIA term for the Agency's business ventures that provided "deep cover" for non-official staff agents and contractors. I figured I didn't need to know any of that yet, because the CIA was omniscient and omnipresent, and everything would just happen, magically, as if according to some perfect plan.

I arrived at the Tucson airport on a Sunday afternoon. I collected my bag and stood and waited. And waited, and waited. The baggage claim area cleared out, and I found myself alone, looking for that missing piece of the omniscient, perfect plan.

Finally, I realized there had been a communication hiccup, and since I had no idea of my destination—no name, no address, nothing—I'd better get to figuring it out.

While in Vietnam I had traveled frequently on Air America, the CIA's proprietary airline, and I remembered the types of aircraft they flew, including C-46s and C-47s. So I went to a phone booth at the airport and trolled through the Yellow Pages. Logically, methodically, I looked up aviation. I scanned the advertisements for the types of aircraft I remembered from Vietnam. And then I found it. I saw the name of an airpark, "Marana," and I called the number.

A young woman answered. "I am at the Tucson airport," I said. "My name is Jim Hawes. Does that name mean anything to you?" There was a pause. "Just a minute, please," she said.

I stood there in the deserted Tucson airport arrivals lounge, gripping the handle of my increasingly annoying bag and balancing my weight from one foot to the other, the plastic phone receiver beginning to draw sweat from my palm.

Finally, I heard shuffling sounds in the background and the woman's voice in a breathless distance as she spoke my name, "Jim Hawes." And then, deeper in the background, another voice, "Oh, shit!"

The young woman came back on the line suddenly, and in a most competent demeanor she said, "Someone will be there soon. Just wait."

So much for omniscience and perfect plans. It was probably the best, simplest, and cheapest lesson on unrealistic expectations that I would learn in my entire three weeks in the OpsFam course.

The course was basically an orientation designed to familiarize contractors like me with the CIA, its history, organization, and expectations.

Other than my SEAL training, and the ops experience in Vietnam, this was my total education on the Agency prior to my departure for the Congo. Assessments of character and integrity were the critical elements, and everything else I needed for this assignment would have to be learned on the job.

Two weeks later, I was in the Congo.

* * *

I arrived in the capital of Léopoldville on a commercial UTA flight from Paris with $2,500 in cash stuffed in my socks and a quantity of morphine-filled syringes in my bag. I knew there would inevitably be casualties, and CIA Supply and Logistics made sure I had what I needed to help get the job done. Whatever they could do to enhance the prospects for success for those conducting the missions was done without hassle or exaggerated bureaucracy. Their experience and support was impressive, and they knew how to respond to a crisis.

The Léopoldville airport scene was not unlike those I had witnessed at remote locations in Southeast Asia. Disheveled and heavily armed Congolese soldiers littered the arrivals area, patrolling like a posse shaking down the few tourists. Dick Johnson, my CIA contact, met me there and ushered me through immigration and customs without so much as a sideways glance.

Johnson was a big guy, with an intellect to match. He might have become a professional NFL player had it not been for the intrusion of WWII. And I quickly knew that Johnson was a man to trust. He was head of all paramilitary activities in the Congo, including the "air ops." A Marine during the war, now career CIA, he would be my boss. We climbed into a black Land Rover and headed directly to the embassy. He began the briefing almost immediately about how things worked in the Congo.

Johnson managed operations from Léopoldville, which was no small challenge. The only way to be in touch with the remote facilities was through primitive and unreliable communications. And I got the feeling that for someone as conscientious as Johnson, the archaic equipment made it all the more important to him to get a proper evaluation of this SEAL that Headquarters had sent him. He had to know if I could handle the job, and he had to make that judgment quickly. I understood that the job required Naval Special Operations expertise, audacity, imagination, and a healthy appreciation of the sensitivity of the global political ramifications.

Johnson had three days to size me up, and it was solely his call whether or not to accept me as the officer-in-charge or send me back to Headquarters.

I was thrilled by the opportunity, and I made a few things clear that first day. I had no self-doubt about whether I was capable of completing the mission. I wanted to make sure Johnson understood that I was ready to put my skills and experience into practice.

On the ride from the airport, Johnson began to probe into my character, to see who this new member of the team was. He said he could help with some of the obstacles I might encounter, but mostly I'd be on my own. I saw some relief in his face when I seemed to be fine with minimal to no supervision. But how else could I have handled it? I'd be working more than a thousand miles east of Léopoldville, across a mammoth, dense jungle, using a communications infrastructure that ranged from antiquated to nonexistent. It did not occur to him to tell me that first day that our only mode of communication would be Morse code, using one-time pads for encryption. It wouldn't have made any difference even if I had known that ahead of time, because there was nothing I could do about it.

As Johnson and I drove along rutted and potholed roads, jostling over the broken pavement all the way to Léopoldville, he gave me his interpretation of the Congo's violent political atmosphere.

When we finally pulled up in front of the off-white, cement-block structure with the US Embassy symbol in front, he cautioned me: building a navy and interdicting supply lines of the Soviet-bloc-backed rebels was a challenge that could only be met at the scene, not remotely from Léopoldville, or from Washington, DC. How I went about it was up to me. I nodded in agreement. There was no pushback and no questions asked. Johnson smiled as he climbed out of the Land Rover. It was an inaugurating point. I had just passed in-country, Stage One.

I spent three days at the embassy in Léopoldville, a disconcerting adventure. The ambiguity of politics threatened my clearly defined mission. I understood the threats and the nuances of the Cold War and was a good sailor. I had embraced the assignment in the Congo in order to enforce the policies that would advance America's political aspirations and hold the line on communist advances in Central Africa. But I was uninterested in the rhythm of diplomacy and had avoided any identity as a State Department employee. Early on I had given my CIA interviewers a thoroughly honest if not entirely welcome statement: "I'd rather be called a pimp in a two-bit whorehouse than a State Department officer."

The path of "non-State Department cover" was how I preferred to work. I wanted to be at the tip of the spear. That's what SEALs are designed for. Waltzing around with the Ambassador made me feel as though I were taking on the shape and likeness of a State Department functionary. And I knew that the success of my mission would require a different mindset.

Johnson had taken me to the embassy for briefings and to meet Larry

Devlin, the CIA's Chief of Station. Devlin had been an Army captain during WWII. He was recruited to the CIA while studying at Harvard. One of his professors had introduced him to McGeorge Bundy, at that time a prominent member of the Council on Foreign Relations. Bundy would later become National Security Advisor to both Presidents Kennedy and Johnson. Bundy asked Devlin to consider joining the CIA, and he did. After a few years in DC, he was posted to Brussels. When the Congo declared independence in 1960, Devlin went to Léopoldville as the first Chief of Station in the new nation.

In the CIA structure, the Chief of Station works out of the embassy. The job requires "running" the case officers (field agents) and cultivating the fragile relationships with the local intelligence services, which is why the true identity of the Chief of Station is usually declared to the host government. Managing the "intel" is a skill and a curse. If it's done properly, sources stay covered, information flows. If not, it can be dangerous and even deadly. Within the embassy itself, the CIA employees are undercover. They work among the staff but are not identified as belonging to the Agency; they are simply passed off as embassy employees. This is both for their protection and for the Agency's benefit.

Devlin was a very adept operator. He spoke fluent French, the only common language in this country of hundreds of tribal languages and dialects, and he was able to build a first-class network of local sources in the Congo. He'd been in the country, on and off, for five years by the time I arrived and had helped to manage the delicate balance of holding the country together. Wisely and professionally, he made it look as though the Ambassador deserved the credit. It was a trait that would put Devlin in very good stead at the embassy, and it's the way an embassy is supposed to work. The Ambassador is the focus of attention. A good COS subordinates his ego to maximize his effectiveness to the job. I benefited from Devlin's good standing at the embassy because Johnson worked for and was trusted by Devlin, and since I worked for Johnson, that trust was extended to me.

At our first meeting, Ambassador Godley expressed his concerns about building the mercenary navy and any publicity that might potentially prove embarrassing to the government. It appeared as though he had little time for me, which was likely a reflection of his confidence in Devlin and Johnson, and which was just as well given my antipathy to State Department ethos.

Ambassador Godley was polite, professional, but not enthusiastic about my mission despite the fact that he knew it was necessary. He'd been in on the planning and had approved the assignment. He gave me no specific direction, except to emphasize the importance of maintaining the covert nature of the mission.

The Ambassador's chief concern was the imported Cuban personnel who were arriving soon. A contingent of Castro's fighters was already working alongside the Soviet-bloc backed Simba Rebels, and injecting anti-Castro Cubans on the other side was a difficult notion for the Ambassador, and State Department officials, to accept. These Cubans were proven fighters who had worked previous missions with Tom Clines, Bill Hamilton's deputy chief of the Maritime Operations Branch, and they would be essential to the mission because they would train the mercenary navy crews. But the concern about their participation was State Department-wide, because they were anti-Castro Cubans, and we would bring them into the country clandestinely and ship them back out, leaving no trace. It was a significant logistical hurdle for the Agency, but I faced a more imposing one first: establishing a base of operations for us to work from.

* * *

I left Léopoldville aboard a paramilitary C-46 cargo plane, owned by a Luxembourg company named WIGMO (Western International Ground Maintenance Organization), the Agency's proprietary airline. It was the only mode of transport across that vast jungle and flew daily supply and courier runs.

The Albertville airport consisted of a single paved tarmac runway with a Quonset hut terminal. And the only other aircraft there were propeller-driven T-28s and a few reconditioned World War II B-26K bombers that all belonged to the Congolese Air Force, flown by the Cuban pilots.

The one road from the airport led directly into town, where mostly boarded-up businesses and a few seedy pubs made up the entire commercial area along the main street. The only industry was a brewery producing a beer labeled "Simba," adding a touch of irony in light of the campaigns of murder, rape, and pillage the Simba Rebels had conducted in the area.

I began to learn everything in this operation would be different. My SEAL training and Vietnam experience included highly skilled professionals and state-of-the-art resources immediately at hand. In the military, I'd also been accustomed to a formal structure of working with other troops and adhering to a coordinated strategy. And where Vietnam may have been the precedent for this new, practical realty, this was a remote enterprise where I went from high-tech to no-tech. There were no historical "how-to's" and no one with previous experience to give me direction or assistance. Once in Albertville, I was completely on my own. No one was there to meet me. No crew existed, and the few available boats were in need of substantial repair. In this remote corner of Africa, the CIA just expected me to handle things on my own and go out and get the job done. That's exactly what I did.

Finding and modifying the warehouse had been just the first and simplest example of operating solo. The building was a leftover relic from a time when the Belgians still owned the Congo and were bleeding the country dry. It was accessed only via an elevated boardwalk that jutted 200 meters into the lake from the port town of Albertville, and it was badly in need of repair.

Since the Belgians had fled the country, the old warehouse didn't belong to anyone anymore. There was no one to pay rent to and no property manager or landlord. I had simply taken it over. We would need it to house parts and a supply inventory and to conduct routine maintenance. The Navy needed sustainability. So, the first job was to get the warehouse protected and minimize the opportunity for theft of the difficult-to-obtain spare parts. I found some local workers, Congolese machinists and carpenters, who had been trained by the Belgians to keep the Port of Albertville functioning. They got the warehouse in order, secured the doors, and shored up the walls, prepping the building for the action to come.

In this location, the "fleet" would be conveniently docked within twenty-five meters of the warehouse, tied up alongside the quay. The quay, on which the warehouse sat, jutted out into the harbor and served as a breakwater against dangerous high seas. This base would prove to be a convenient location to launch a naval patrol or an assault in support of the 5 Commando mercenary army.

By the time repairs began on the warehouse, I had started to define my territory. I knew that word had got around that I was remaking everything, including recruiting a navy that would be commanded by an American. And it was evident from the "git-go" that LCol Hoare, as head of the mercenary army, wouldn't be happy to relinquish any aspect of his command. He saw me as a junior officer, even though I operated under the assumed rank of "commander," a Navy rank that I did not claim, but was attributed to me. It was equivalent to Hoare's army rank of lieutenant colonel. The ruse worked to the Navy's advantage, so I allowed it to be perpetuated. I had recognized early on that I absolutely could not share command or responsibility for the success of the interdiction mission of the Congo's new Navy, the "Force Navale Congolaise."

I knew that Dick Johnson was the quality of boss who would support my decision, as long as it was for the right reasons. In this case, the interdiction of weapons and supplies to the rebels was the priority; the support of Hoare's troops the secondary mission.

My suspicions were soon confirmed that LCol Hoare would have a difficult time adjusting to the idea that I didn't report to him. I was about to step into his territory and he wasn't accustomed to relinquishing control to anyone. For the sake of smooth coordination of operations between the Army and the Navy, however, I had to make sure that my actions would convince him that separate command would not inhibit the effectiveness of his ground forces, but instead would make them better.

* * *

After my encounter with the 5 Commandos and assisting them with breaking into their safe, and once I secured a base of operations at the commandeered warehouse, I returned to the Hotel Du Lac where I'd checked in earlier that morning. This would be my new home for the unforeseeable future, and Lake Tanganyika shimmered several hundred yards off to the east. My first night at the hotel I tried to settle in. I wrung the sweat from my shirt, rinsed it out, and hung it up to drip dry in the bathroom. I opened a cold beer and walked out onto the balcony overlooking the main thoroughfare in Albertville.

A feverish August breeze came up off the lake as the street below began to fill up. A parade of women and children, led by priests and missionaries, in triple and quadruple file, dressed in vibrantly patterned, mismatched skirts and blouses, created a scene like a kaleidoscope revolving beneath my balcony. The women swayed in an orderly procession between the century palms lining Main Street. Some carried infants swaddled to their backs, and many were adorned with distinctly colored headdresses. They carried sticks and cans containing stones and tins to bang on—anything to produce a beat and provide a rhythm for the parade. It was spectacular in its creativity.

I leaned back, took in the air and the spectacle, and began to sketch out a design to build a navy out of no-tech resources and second-rate troops.

Chapter Six

Recruiting a Cutthroat

The event that contributed more than any other toward the success of the Force Navale Congolaise was the recruitment of 5 Commando's Regimental Sergeant Major ("RSM") Samuel "Jock" Cassidy. He had trained every 5 Commando mercenary in the country and was a hardened soldier of fortune. A veteran of Congo and mercenary warfare, the key to his real value was the personnel files he held in his head. Acquiring Cassidy, with his knowledge and assessment of the troops, meant that I'd be able to recruit the best of the mercenaries. And if I could do that, I'd assemble a Navy with the capabilities to accomplish this mission.

Cassidy had been away on medical leave, and when he returned I sent a message to him to meet me at the Hotel Du Lac. The liberty I was taking in allowing a presumed rank higher than the one I held was going to be an asset in this meeting with Cassidy. I needed to convey a sense of leadership of this emerging Navy by allowing people to believe I was a Commander, instead of a twenty-six-year-old Lieutenant (Junior Grade, not even a full Lieutenant Senior Grade). But within this off-the-grid, quasi-military Congo structure, as Johnson predicted, I was facing a situation that required grit and considerable acting skills.

Cassidy was older than I was, and I knew him as a murderer and a plunderer with a hair-trigger that often led to violence. He was tough, mean-tough, and the word on him was that he had racked up a catalogue of savage acts that had earned the fear of every mercenary working in the Congo, and many other parts of Africa. Cassidy's mood swings and foul temper were legendary, and rumored to be caused by a bad liver, which I believe was the reason he'd been away on medical leave. I'd heard that his health problems were brought on by the wicked combination of tropical diseases, contaminated water, and too much booze. He was paranoid when drunk, which he was much of the time, although never when he was on duty. He still looked very sickly when I met him that first afternoon.

Instinctively, I addressed him as if he were a UDT/SEAL trainee, which was a direct line back to the year I spent as an instructor. Thank you, Captain Lee.

"We're going to build a navy," I told him. "With or without you. But if you come on board, together we will make an effective force in this war." I forced him to stand as if he were a subordinate officer and he stared at me with a lacerating glare.

"I know you're a mercenary," I continued, "but I will not bid against LCol Hoare for your services." I was in my element and I felt as though I had the upper hand in this conversation, because I had a desirable card to play. So I sweetened the pot. "What I will do," I told him, "is see to it that you are commissioned a Lieutenant, and if you are as good as you are reputed to be, and I believe you are, I'll make you Captain." I paused a moment to let this sink in.

I had this planned out. I wanted to maintain the army ranks, and not introduce Navy ranks, as the mercenaries were all officially still a part of 5 Commando. I knew that as RSM he was the senior non-commissioned officer of the 5 Commando regiment, and I sensed that being a commissioned officer was important to him. It was a status Cassidy would never receive from Hoare, because he had more value to Hoare as his RSM of the regiment.

I didn't smile, I didn't offer him my hand. I casually glanced out the window of the Du Lac and pretended to be distracted by some children playing on the veranda. Then I turned back to Cassidy. "You have a decision to make," I said. His eyes narrowed, and I couldn't tell if it was fury or deliberation.

I forged ahead as if I had all the power, as though this "recruit's" future were up to me, just like a wannabe SEAL back at Little Creek. "Now you can either come on board, or pack your kit and get out." I paused, but not for long. "What is your decision?"

There was an extended and uncomfortably silent moment where I thought I might have miscalculated this maneuver. And I didn't have a backup plan if he refused. I would have to regroup.

Finally, Cassidy nodded in agreement. He didn't smile and didn't act like he'd just made the best decision of his career. But he accepted my proposition and signed on to the Navy, luckily for me. As I would later learn, because of that direct confrontation I could have become a victim of Cassidy's erratic temper, as others had in the past and would in the future. And instead of acquiring a captain for the Navy I might have ended up with a bullet my head.

Weeks later, after we clearly saw how effective we could be together as a team, Cassidy finally gave me his impression of this initial meeting. "Commander," he said, "I trained every mercenary in 5 Commando, and no one, including LCol Hoare, ever talked to me the way you did that first day. I didn't know whether to join you or kill you. Lucky for us both, I signed on." Once again the old adage, "better lucky than good," proved valid. Whatever his reasoning, we were now a working team and we set our sights on assembling a Congo Navy.

Over the course of the next months, Cassidy would become exceptionally loyal to me; or more accurately, at least as loyal as he was capable of being. I could give him something that mattered to him, a military status that he wanted and believed he might never achieve: a commission. So together we began our troop recruitment and started to mold them into sailors.

The loss of his Regimental Sergeant Major had infuriated LCol Hoare, but the Navy was autonomous from Hoare's command and there was nothing he could do about it.

"Mad" Mike Hoare was a first-class actor. The clear evidence of this comes from the CIA Station Chief Larry Devlin's own assessment. Devlin was both intellectually tough and physically brave, and referred to Hoare as a "gentleman adventurer," a characterization that might cover a variety of traits including bandit, which he was, according to Cassidy. During our time together, Cassidy confided in me that he and another officer in 5 Commando, John Peters, were tasked with securing Hoare's share of anything they looted or stole from the banks, vaults, and safes in every town they hit in the Congo. I wasn't aware at the time, but the rumor within 5 Commando was that Cassidy himself was sitting on a large stash of gold that he and the others had managed to steal from the mines in the area surrounding Watsa, a gold mining operation in the Northeast Congo.

LCol Hoare's transition to adventurer came out of unlikely circumstances. Like many people who have lived a bland life, Hoare's personal history might seem obscure and nondescript, right up to the point where he first gained notoriety, and that happened in the Congo.

He was born in India, served in Lord Mountbatten's staff in World War II in the British Army in South Asia, and had been educated as a chartered accountant; hardly rigorous prerequisites for a mercenary commander. But through a friend, he was introduced to the one of the Congo's most powerful political figures, Moise Tshombe, the Governor of the breakaway Katanga Province, and once he was in, he took full advantage.

Some of his critics would label Hoare a puppet, which is far from accurate. Hoare's ability to act his role was crucial to commanding a mercenary army, particularly because he had no formal judicial recourse structure. What he did have was good fundamental military skills, and that meant he could recognize those same skills in others and employ them accordingly.

He masterfully played the "above the riff-raff" role of a British gentleman-officer. Tapped to lead mercenary troops in overcoming a communist threat, his theater of war was a small but important strategic part of the Cold War world. He had an acute sense for both strategy and tactics, and I saw him juggle cold-blooded killers, African leaders, and US Embassy employees with aplomb, while still focusing on chasing down and destroying the rebels.

Also, he was lucky. Hoare had Belgian Colonel Hardenne, Chief of Staff "Ops Sud" (Operations South) as a quasi-boss. Hardenne coordinated between the Congolese Army and the mercenaries. A high-minded and competent Belgian officer, he was a "get the mission accomplished regardless of who gets the credit" type of military leader. I saw Hoare benefit from Hardenne's exemplary character more than once, and Hoare was always happy to get the credit.

We had daily operations meetings at 16:00, except during campaigns. A bit ragged and contentious in the beginning, the meetings became focused and productive once Hoare clearly understood the Navy's value and my determination to be cooperative and supportive.

Initially, it was a bitter pill for him to swallow that he wouldn't be commanding the Navy, but he came to realize we would make it possible for him to get his job done. The Navy would be as available as the interdiction mission permitted, and that would make Hoare look good, which suited him right down to the ground. The meeting agendas always included strategies on how the Navy could best reinforce Army movements with gunfire support, and by troop landings on the lakeshore beaches. The rebels were well entrenched in these lakeside enclaves and we were going to do our best to identify the sites and cut off the supplies the rebels desperately needed. We plotted and continually revised tactics on how the Navy would break those supply lines.

In time, after it became apparent that the new arrangement actually made his efforts more effective, Hoare accepted the separate command structure. And throughout the following months, our daily meetings became essential as the pace and complexity of the operations increased. Cassidy attended the meetings on occasion and helped review operations and plan new ones.

With Cassidy's stature among the mercenaries, and extra incentives I was able to include, we got the toughest and smartest from the ranks of the 5 Commando. But in that context, "toughest" and "smartest" had its own definition—most brutal and conniving is probably more accurate.

The recruits assumed there was a prospect of American military might sustaining our work, and consequently Cassidy had little trouble convincing the men we selected from Hoare's command to come on board. But another more critical motivation would be the tangible ingredient that assisted us in rustling Hoare's men over to the Navy.

It was a 1910-vintage Lake Tanganyika steamer, the *Kivu*. It wasn't sexy, but it became a recruiting magnet.

Several of these 3,000 to 5,000-ton lake steamers were idle, no longer sailing in trans-lake commerce. Berthed and tied up at the quay, the fifty-year-old *Kivu* was destined to become the Navy's barracks barge and mess.

The *Kivu*'s value as a recruiting tool became apparent to me early on. For anyone considering switching over to our Navy, the attraction of a dry, comfortable place to sleep was a major factor. The mercenary army, the ground-pounders, slept rough and ate bad. Lousy food, plenty of bugs, and crude latrines were the norm for these soldiers. Our steamer offered shelter, a "rack" (bed), a clean mess hall with decent food, some security, and one other important element: status. Cassidy, as Mess Captain, could ensure cleanliness and sanitation to a degree not possible in the Army. Eat well, sleep clean—a perfect recipe for recruitment.

I had no cash for the purchase of assets, so the maneuver to acquire the *Kivu* to house the troops would have to be an aggressive one, similar to the acquisition of the warehouse operating base.

One sweltering morning I stood on the dock with a contingent of my newly-hired men, all of them armed. We moved up the gangplank and simply boarded the *Kivu*, advancing en masse to the wheelhouse where we found the stunned "captain," a young Congolese sailor. With the armed mercenaries standing on all sides of me, I pulled a piece of paper out of my pocket and wrote out an IOU and showed it to the bewildered sailor. "The US Government owes you $5,000 US for one vessel," it read. I included a description of the ship and the fact that it was commandeered by the Force Navale Congolaise for use on Lake Tanganyika, and then I stared him in the eyes before I dated and signed it, "James M. Hawes, Officer of the United States of America."

Roughly a dollar a ton for a half-antique, out-of-service vessel seemed a fair price to pay. It was a melodramatic and probably unnecessary display of force. But it worked. The "captain" and crew marched off the ship and we took charge of the *Kivu*. As far as I know, no one has ever attempted to collect on that IOU.

Cassidy, as Captain of the Mess, designated one man as the provisions person, a "go-fer" who would arrange and "go-fer" supplies and act as errand-boy. Since each mercenary in the Navy contributed from his pay to the "mess," they all had a stake in maintaining an ongoing food supply. When Cassidy discovered that the go-fer had embezzled from the mess, a breach in the standard of conduct, Cassidy dispensed a form of punishment that was the most extreme, pressurized bullying tactic I had ever witnessed. His ruthless form of discipline would give apoplexy to the US Navy and the UCMJ (Uniform Code of Military Justice). It was a glaring example of the difference between a proper military and this mercenary force.

The cold locker on the fifty-year-old ship was equipped with thick, insulated walls, built when ice was the only available cooling system. Over the years of misuse and abuse it had deteriorated to the point that it was now inhabited by rats and squadrons of creepy-crawly, biting creatures that thrive in a dark and damp equatorial environment.

When Cassidy discovered the larceny by his hand-picked go-fer, the Captain of the Mess called the Navy into formation. This misappropriation would have been a petty concern when compared to some of Cassidy's own non-Navy escapades that I was aware of, but nonetheless, he stood the men at attention as the pilferer's crime was announced. "This man stole from the mess," he declared.

And with that, Cassidy threw the man into the cold storage locker and bolted the door.

Twenty-four hours later, Cassidy again assembled the men at attention. He brought the criminal out of cold storage, considerably less perky after spending a day and night in pitch dark, solitary confinement in the company of disease-carrying vermin and blood-sucking insects. Cassidy made the identical announcement as the previous day, "This man stole from the mess." And he threw the man back in.

The scene was repeated the following day. With the men at attention, Cassidy pulled the go-fer from his confines. Only now the man's body had begun to physically jerk and spasm, and it's possible he was hallucinating. He swatted at unseen creatures flying over his head. Cassidy made his announcement, "This man stole from the mess," and again threw the guy back into the hellhole.

On day three, after seventy-two hours of no food and minimal water, Cassidy produced the man and the histrionics were repeated. Only now the go-fer was nearly insane, completely broken. Three days in the sodden dungeon, battling real and imaginary demons, had taken its toll. Cassidy stood back and allowed his men a long, thought-provoking look at the wretch before them. Then he pointed at the thief and shouted, "This man stole from the mess! No one will ever steal from the mess again." And none of those thieves ever did.

Chapter Seven

Logistics Genius

I was settled into the three-story Hotel Du Lac at that point, in a room on the top floor at the front. From that vantage point I could see all the way down to the harbor and was able to keep an eye on the boats.

The owners of the Du Lac were a Greek family that had endured repeated brutality during the persistent rebel raids on the area. And for some unfathomable reason, they had not been murdered.

Perhaps the rebels calculated that if they ever took permanent control of the town they'd need a hotel and hotel operators. The Greek family was caught in the endless cycle of political and civil unrest. Albertville was the only home they had and even though the violence was a catalyst to leave, there were no buyers for their only asset, a low-tariff hotel in this rebel-infested region. But they ran the place with pride. It was a clean establishment that served a decent meal even during the sparse weeks when food supplies weren't readily available.

It was a five- or ten-minute walk to what would be our Navy yard. Some days I would take the time out to peer into the Bata Shoe Store, which was the only business left standing that had an intact glass window front.

The rest of the town was shuttered, except for a couple of sleazy bars that attracted my curiosity but never enough for me to walk inside. One of them was the Bar Kalemie, which would become well known to me later in my time in Albertville. But those bars were not my territory and I knew I had enough risks to juggle without pursuing more.

The port was only barely operational. A small amount of dockside work was going on, and the cranes functioned only adequately. They would serve a critical function for Navy requirements, because the boats needed to be berthed, maintained, and supplied out of that port. Routine maintenance in the work areas had deteriorated with the escalation in the fighting, but the skills of the Congolese machinists I had found to shore up the warehouse were a testament to what must have been a quality training program when the Belgians were in charge. The machinists' expertise was high in comparison to their education, which was minimal.

It took me a little time working in Albertville to understand that the commerce on and around Lake Tanganyika was dominated by the Greek community. Ricardo Chavez reported many times throughout his ship's log that he and his crew frequently found small coveys of fishing boats working the lake at night or early in the morning. The boats were almost always captained by Greek fishermen.

The enterprise creativity of this group was impressive, which was also the case with the Greek family that ran the Hotel Du Lac. These immigrants had settled in the Congo and made up part of this network of Greeks who carved out a living there. Many of those who fished the lake were based out of Albertville and their unofficial leader seemed to be one of the younger fellows, an extremely likeable and creative man named Tasos Maillis.

The fishing fleet would often bring in a magnificent catch of Nile perch, a large freshwater fish that is native to the Congo. The fish would get fat feasting on a moth that had a monthly life-cycle and was so prolific that it would cover the lake and make it look briefly like there was snow in the tropics.

I asked a group of fishermen to introduce me to Tasos. He was an unforgettable character, optimistic and industrious. He had purchased the fishing fleet for pennies on the dollar from the Belgians who had fled when the first shots were fired and the rebels began their brutal assaults. Many of the Belgian owners lost heart and decided to flee the constant threat of violence and uncertainty. Tasos had stepped right in and purchased the fleet and expanded it by building more boats, which he did pretty much single-handedly.

Tasos was happily married to a Belgian woman he'd met in Katanga, who was accustomed to the rigors of life in that no-frills environment. She delivered a daughter in Albertville—no hospital, no obstetrician, just nature—and never gave it a second thought. They made a good couple. She was helpful in the business, supportive and uncomplaining, and in return, Tasos was very attentive and appreciative.

He had converted a few narrow-gauge railroad cars to refrigerated cars and created long-range, international Lake Tanganyika shipping commerce, moving chilled and frozen fish, including Nile perch. Tasos's network serviced every community by rail all the way to Elisabethville (now Lubumbashi), the capital of Katanga Province. He then expanded his business to include dried fish and sold that to the local communities in the immediate vicinity of Albertville.

He moved freight and goods around the lake to Kigoma, in Tanganyika, Bujumbura, in Burundi, and smaller ports along both coasts of the lake. And when I learned that, my immediate thought was, "this is a built-in intelligence net."

I invited Tasos to visit the base of operations for the Force Navale Congolaise. I took him in tow and showed him what we had at the time and explained the kind of operation we were trying to build. At the base, there were a few old Seacrafts stacked against the warehouse parts and maintenance area. They were pretty well shot up and of no use to me. Tasos asked what I intended to do with these hulls. I replied, "Nothing. They can't be repaired, and we're bringing in different types of boats with different type engines."

Tasos asked me if he could have one of the hulls. I agreed, but told him to just make sure that it could not be attributed to the US government. I remember giving him the spare engine parts because I knew we wouldn't be needing them.

Tasos was extremely grateful for this, and asked what he could do for me in return. I relied, "Just help keep me alive. Let me know what's going on around the lake." Tasos took that as a given, but also kept trying to repay me in some way.

Finally, when I realized he wasn't going to stop asking about repaying the favor, I confessed that I really liked baklava (a delicious Greek honey and nut pastry). I was certain there was no way that Tasos could deliver on that, but I didn't know him well enough at that point to understand just how resourceful he was. Also, I was not aware that Olympic Airways flew from Athens to Johannesburg and made a stop in Elisabethville along the way.

Tasos arranged to have a baklava placed onboard in Athens, and then he had it collected in Elisabethville and somehow delivered to Albertville. Needless to say, I was surprised, very pleasantly, and thoroughly enjoyed that baklava for its short lifespan. It was a classic expression of the man that Tasos was.

In the end, it was a very favorable exchange, that old broken-out boat bottom and useless spare parts for authentic Greek baklava. And I never gave another thought to that hull until years later.

One day Tasos came to me with an idea and I wanted to help him out. He was trying to build a fishmeal plant in Albertville. I thought it sounded like a solid business plan and I offered to contact the Fisheries Attaché at the US Embassy in Abidjan, Ivory Coast. I sent a telegram identifying myself, introducing Tasos and the concept of a fishmeal plant, and suggesting that when the attaché next visited the Congo that he meet with Tasos and evaluate this opportunity, which seemed to be very beneficial to the local economy.

Not long after that my boss contacted me via a single sideband radio, Johnson in Léopoldville, me in Albertville. Dick said to me, "What is this about a fishmeal plant? We got a message here at the embassy from the Fisheries Attaché in Abidjan, inquiring about you and a telegram you sent."

Of course, as I related the story I could visualize him shaking his head. Because even to me at that point it seemed pretty far off my mission statement. Finally, Johnson said, "Jim, you are there to prosecute a war. Forget fishmeal plants. Understand?" I replied, "Yes, sir," and that was the end of the fishmeal venture. It was too bad though. It was a well-thought-out plan and I'm certain Tasos could have pulled it off successfully. He was that good.

Over the months I spent in Albertville, Tasos and I became very good friends. He continually funneled information to me that he and his fishing crews had picked up. They were in every community up and down the lake, and their knowledge of the area and the people contributed intelligence we never could have obtained on our own. He was my "inside guy."

Subsequently, through information his fishing fleet had gathered, Tasos was able to tell me when the Simbas would open new camps on the beaches along the eastern shore of the lake. This was critical information that let us in on where and how the enemy received their weapons and supplies. It was insider stuff that became an ongoing asset for our interdiction efforts. I've never disclosed Tasos's intelligence gathering until now. In addition to becoming a lifelong friend, Tasos was a very lucky find, an on-the-ground resource for me in

Albertville. When I departed at the end of my assignment, I was sorry to have lost contact with him. But we would find each other again a few years later.

* * *

Things were beginning to fall into place. With Tasos's help, we had our intelligence network. Our base was defined, Cassidy was on board as the operational commander and enthusiastic about his "command," our recruitment of would-be sailors was underway, and the barracks and mess was arranged. The boats on hand were being repaired, and our Navy was launched. We were ready to move to the next phase.

Our primary focus now had to be on the boats. The craft currently in the Congo were in poor shape and inadequate for the mission that the Navy had been asked to accomplish. Headquarters, with input from Dick Johnson and me, had been working on this planned expansion of the Navy.

We had a few smaller boats, exaggeratedly termed "PTs," which were operated from the *Ermans*, the 250-ton lake vessel that we'd inherited from McKay and had commandeered for the Navy. We called the *Ermans* "the Mothership." She was the command operations vessel for the PTs and armed with captured Russian weapons, including 12.7mm Russian machine guns and a US 75mm recoilless rifle.

The *Ermans* was also equipped with a Decca radar and line-of-sight radios that would vector the PTs to targets on the lake identified on the radar. If we determined that those targets needed inspection and/or interdiction, the *Ermans* could also provide plenty of heavy armament capabilities.

Altogether, it was a solid battery of munitions we put to good use in offshore gunfire support for the Army's lakeshore landings. But we needed fortified boats that could quickly identify, pursue, and engage the enemy in sustained firefights on the water, and Washington would come through.

Peter Jessup of the National Security staff wrote a memo to President Johnson stating that "a more substantial pocket Coast Guard is necessary." He made it clear that the 303 Committee approved "the purchase, transport by air, and armament and manning of six additional boats (two Swifts and four Seacrafts)."

With that 303 Committee order, we had six Seacrafts, which were inboard-outboard water-ski type craft, comparable to the popular Boston Whaler, on which we'd mount a .30 caliber machine gun forward and a shoulder-fired 3.5-inch rocket launcher (bazooka) aft. But it was the two Swift Boats—and who crewed them—that made all the difference in our mission.

The Swifts, fifty-foot aluminum diesel-powered boats, were developed in Louisiana as a "water taxi" to deliver equipment and crews to the offshore oil-rigs in the Gulf of Mexico. Subsequently, the DOD modified them to US Navy specifications and tailored them for coastal patrols and riverine warfare in Vietnam. They had a maximum speed of twenty-five knots, were a shallow-draft patrol craft that was fast, reliable, and sturdy, and they could carry weapons. In the Congo, we would make further modifications to these boats. They were meant to be the rapid, versatile centerpiece of our Congo Navy. Once we could get the Swifts and properly trained sailors to crew them, we were going to be the dominant force on the lake. The only problem was how to get them to the Congo.

Logistically, we faced significant obstacles. This was a clandestine operation, so a conventional solution was not an option. We needed a way to get a crew and transport these boats, and do it in a hurry. The Swift Boat is just over fifty feet in length and weighs nearly 37,000 pounds. Getting two of them into the Congo would require radical measures and a good deal of lateral thinking. Solving that dilemma would become one of the most complex and ingenious enterprises of our assignment.

* * *

Here Bill Hamilton, the Chief of the CIA's Maritime Branch of the Special Operations Group, comes back in the picture. As he had recommended me for the Congo job, I was well aware of his stellar accomplishments and credentials. But in order to get the Congo Navy operation under way, Hamilton and his deputy, Tom Clines, had to create an ambitious and innovative scheme.

Hamilton had known Fred Sewart, who was the owner of Sewart Seacraft, the company that manufactured the Swifts. Sewart Seacraft had been in the boat manufacturing business for many years, building craft that were meant to service the offshore oil industry in the Gulf of Mexico. The company enjoyed a superb reputation.

Hamilton went to Morgan City, Louisiana, Sewart's then base of operations, to meet with Sewart and organize a boat delivery to the Congo.

Hamilton knew that there were two Swift Boats that had recently been operating out of Nicaragua, manned by Cuban exiles who were running raids against Castro's navy. These Cuban fighters had been carefully selected for their experience in maritime operations, and particularly with the Swift Boats. I believe Hamilton may have purchased those Swifts from Sewart for that purpose. Hamilton and Clines developed a plan to transfer those same Swift Boats from the Caribbean to the Congo.

The CIA had backed an anti-Castro maritime force that was running raids out of Central America. They were known as the MRR, *Movimiento Recuperación Revolucionaria* (Revolutionary Recovery Movement). Headed by Manuel Artime, the boat crews were working throughout the Caribbean, running down and attacking ships in Castro's navy. In early 1964, the Cuban exiles had received those two-brand new Swift Boats, named the *Monty* and the *Gitana*, compliments of the CIA.

Ricardo Chavez was the captain of the *Monty*, and Santiago Alvarez, Jr., captained the *Gitana*. Roberto Pichardo was the communications specialist. This band of trained military operators set up their first base in Puerto Limon, Costa Rica. But it was a semi-busy port and the Cubans quickly determined they were attracting too much attention there. They decided to find a new location.

They sailed north and settled on Monkey Point, a deserted strip of beach bound by dense jungle just across the border in Nicaragua. They initially slept in tents, with no other facilities whatsoever, and eventually carved out a paramilitary base there. Within a few days others arrived to help establish the base. Eulogio "Papo" Reyes, along with Generoso Bringas, Serapio Cepedo, and about a dozen others, were the first to establish that Cuban raiding team.

Together they hacked away at the jungle, chopping down overgrown trees and clearing wild vegetation to establish an undercover camp on the edge of the tropical Nicaraguan jungle. By the fall of 1964, there were nearly 170 men working at Monkey Point in a well-equipped, dynamic paramilitary base.

The Swifts arrived several weeks later. Chavez and another operative working for the CIA named Jorge Arroyo delivered the boats from the base in Costa Rica. They had left Puerto Limon and sailed a short distance to Nicaragua just north of the Tortuguero River on the border. And even though the boats were brand new, they would get specially authorized radar gear.

Chavez was trained on radar in Louisiana by Edwin Wilson, who, following an illustrious career, became an infamous rogue CIA operative. Convicted in 1983 of illegally selling weapons to Libya, Wilson spent twenty-two years in prison, most of that time in solitary confinement. Wilson's conviction was overturned and he was released from prison in 2004 when the US District Court Judge for the Southern District of Texas wrote a scathing opinion finding that the US Department of Justice and the CIA had covered up and withheld evidence in the case. In their zeal to prosecute, they effectively framed a guilty man.

In the earlier days of his extensive maritime career, Wilson had acquired a preference for Decca equipment, a preference that proved very valuable to us. Wilson had that brand of radar brought to Monkey Point to be installed on the Swifts by Pichardo, who arrived there about the same time as the *Monty* and *Gitana*. Pichardo's firsthand knowledge of the newly installed radar gear would make him an exceptionally useful electronics technician when the operation moved to the Congo. He would know the equipment intimately, having designed and organized the installation from scratch.

Chavez and Artime took charge of the base in Nicaragua and set up an operation out of which they would run the sabotage missions against Castro's Communists.

In September 1964, an incident on the Caribbean triggered the events that would result in the redeployment of the *Monty* and *Gitana* to the Congo, more than six thousand miles away.

A nighttime attack on a Spanish cargo vessel, the *Sierra Aránzazu*, carrying goods bound for Cuba, would signal the end of the MRR's raids. The Spanish ship was mistaken for the Cuban vessel the *Sierra Maestra*. Someone in the crew identified only the name "Sierra" on the fantail of the Spanish vessel, and believing it was the *Sierra Maestra*, the ship was attacked. Three crew members were killed and the ship was set afire and sank. The remaining seventeen crew members abandoned the burning vessel and were picked up by the Dutch ship *P. G. Thulin*.

Following that event, the Johnson administration pulled the funds for the MRR and their Caribbean operations were brought to an end. The Cuban exiles spent approximately another month at the base in Nicaragua before they all returned to Miami.

Hamilton and Clines must have had a revelation about how to fulfill the newly authorized and funded Congo Navy mission. With the *Monty* and *Gitana* "decommissioned" from the anti-Castro maritime raids, they were available, equipped with special radar and radios, and in nearly new condition. Their crews were well trained, disciplined, and devoted to combating communism across the globe. Both fit our cause perfectly.

The training cadre for my Navy would be made up of these extremely brave and experienced Cuban-exile naval personnel who deserve much of the credit for our success in the Congo. Among this group of Cuban exiles who had previously worked with Clines over the years was Ricardo Chavez. He would be my team leader. Clines had garnered loyalty from Chavez and his men, so his recommendation carried deserved credibility. They were on board.

Clines would turn the Cuban contingent over to me with a message: "These men are tough, resourceful, and brave, and take pride in their performance. But above all else, they're loyal. Chavez is a proven leader and the men believe in him. So there will be no discipline problems. Over the years we have developed a trusting relationship based on shared experiences. And I am assigning these bonds of trust and friendship over to you."

When he endorsed and transferred expectations to me, I received a team prepared to work unconditionally under my command, no questions asked.

"You're all set," Clines told me. "Now, don't fuck it up."

* * *

Our boats and our crew were committed. The complication was transporting them to the Congo.

Ours was a clandestine mission, so it had to be done with stealth. The boats were too small to sail across the Atlantic Ocean, and too large to transport overland through multiple countries to Lake Tanganyika. And shipping them commercially as cargo didn't fit into the clandestine nature of the scheme. Hamilton's and Cline's solution was both innovative and shrewd. But first the *Monty* and the *Gitana* had to be brought back to Louisiana.

A small crew of the Cuban exiles returned to Monkey Point in Nicaragua, boarded the Swifts, and prepared them to sail through the Gulf of Mexico and to be delivered to Morgan City, Louisiana, where Hamilton and Clines were waiting and would take charge of them.

Chavez captained the *Monty* and Alvarez the *Gitana*, just as they always had. They sailed north along Central America and in keeping with the still clandestine nature of their work, stopped and gassed up the boats at a small Mexican island called Isla Mujeres just off the Yucatan Peninsula near Cancun. From there they were supposed to head straight to the southern coast of Louisiana. But a few miles off shore all the engines on both the Swifts began to sputter. Engineman Papo Reyes recalls, "I had trouble with the engine, all the way I had trouble, oh my god."

They made the shorter sail across the gulf to Naples, Florida, where they discovered there had been water in the diesel fuel they'd purchased in Mexico. The fuel filters on all four engines had to be changed and new diesel purchased. Reyes was furious with the Mexicans. "After we left Naples, no more trouble, we got into the gulf and got to Morgan Town (sic)."

By the time they arrived in Louisiana, the Cubans were frustrated and just handed the boats over. "I said to Manolo (Artime), I don't want to sleep in Morgan Town, I just want to go to Miami. And I flew back to Miami the same night."

If the challenge in acquiring the Swifts for the Congo operation was about transporting them, the solution was surgery. They made the decision to cut the two Swifts into pieces, strip out the engines, load all the parts onto US military transport planes, and fly them to the Congo.

But it wasn't as simple as "take 'em apart and put 'em back together." There was no one in the Congo who was even remotely qualified to execute, let alone oversee, such an operation. Consequently, on both continents, the task fell onto the Cajun boat builders who worked at Sewart Seacraft.

Lobert Broussard had worked at Sewart for sixteen years when Bill Hamilton arrived there that summer. Broussard recalls that the company owner, Fred

Sewart, called him into the office to meet the "big guy," meaning Hamilton. According to Broussard, they "shot the bull" for a little while until Hamilton got up and went to a board at the front of the room. There he drew a picture of the continent of Africa, and on the central portion, he placed an X over the location of Lake Tanganyika. Then he sat down. Broussard remembers that Hamilton told him, "We'd like for you to go over there and bring some boats."

Hamilton leaned in, and with the serious tone of a man accustomed to working on clandestine "ops," he cautioned Broussard, telling him that the operation was completely secret and Broussard was not to tell anyone about it.

They estimated that he'd have to be gone about two months. But Broussard hesitated. "I'm not going to leave my wife for that long and not tell her. So she's gotta know," he protested. With a nod of approval from his boss, Ken Hidalgo, Hamilton agreed to allow Broussard to tell his wife.

Under the supervision of Chief Designer Hidalgo, the dismantling of the Swifts began. The first thing Broussard and his team did was to test run the Swifts up and down a canal to check their current running capability. Then they hauled the boats up on the bank and stripped them, removing two engines from each Swift, the Detroit Diesel V-1271's, manufactured by General Motors. The superstructure—the cabin portion of the boats—was separated from the hull and removed, and the hulls were bisected longitudinally. They were pieces of a 37,000-pound aluminum puzzle waiting to be stitched back together.

Every piece was placed onto cradles in the back of Sewart's trucks and then hauled to the airport in New Iberia, Louisiana. "When we had everything at the airport," says Broussard, "they sent the planes."

The segments of the *Monty* and *Gitana* were then loaded into five planes, three C-124s (known as Globemasters) plus two C-130s. The dissection of the boats wasn't enough to fit the pieces onto the aircraft, because the bows on the Swifts were about two feet too long. The remedy was to cut off the bows so that they would fit inside the largest plane.

Our efforts to bring two dismantled Swifts to the Congo had a precedent during World War I when the British Navy, countering German dominance in Africa, transported fighting boats to the Congo. That operation became the inspiration for John Huston's Oscar-winning film *The African Queen* (1951) starring Humphrey Bogart and Katharine Hepburn.

These two works of genius, audacious in their scope, had striking similarities. The American and British boats were nearly the same size. The Swifts were fifty feet, the British craft forty feet. The English used rail, sea, and overland carriage. We had aircraft at our disposal, but otherwise employed the same modes of transport. And they, just like us, needed to stay under the radar, hidden from savvy spies. They were tracked by the Germans; we were watched by the Soviets, Chinese, and Cubans.

Firepower needed beefing up. We and the Brits both added weapons to the boats: .50 caliber machine guns amidships and a recoilless rifle on the stern for our Swifts; Maxim machine guns aft and three-pounder Hotchkiss guns on the bows of the British boats.

And just like ours, their vessels arrived near Albertville, the spot where the Force Navale Congolaise would have its base of operations.

The rewards in both incidences were bankable. Our initial assessment in the Congo found the Simba Rebels enjoying free rein up and down the lake. And in 1915, the German Navy dominated all lake traffic with two sixty-ton gunboats. But by the end of our term, we would severe the Simba lifeline of weapons, food, and supplies on Lake Tanganyika and help end the murderous insurgency. And fifty years earlier, on the very same body of water, the Brits had sunk and destroyed the German East African Fleet.

Two ops, fifty years apart, connected by parallel circumstance, and both on the right side of history.

In our Congo operation there were several concerns about dissecting and transporting the boats: once they were reassembled, would they work? Would they be seaworthy? And could they hold up in combat? We needed to make sure that the answer to all those questions was "yes." And since Sewart's Cajun boat builders were recruited to come along to the Congo with the boats, we'd have more certainty that everything would go smoothly.

A team of six highly skilled Louisiana natives, led by Broussard, accompanied the Swifts and made the journey inside the belly of a C-124s.

The Cajuns are also known as "coonasses," a term to be used among themselves and by their approved friends only. "Coonass" is a glaringly "non-PC" term today—so much so that a concurrent resolution passed by the Louisiana state legislature in 1981 condemned the use of the word, although the 159th

Tactical Fighter Group of the Louisiana Air National Guard was called the "Coonass Militia" until 1992.

But in '65, once we became friends, that's exactly how we referred to them, and how they referred to themselves. And that team of Cajun experts would be asked to reassemble and re-animate our Swifts, on the scene, once they arrived in Albertville.

Bill Hamilton accompanied the Cajuns and together they took the ride in the cargo hold of the planes, flying all the way to Africa alongside the boat parts.

Broussard kept a detailed diary of his adventures, which includes the itinerary. The planes stopped at a naval airbase in Florida and spent the night, then on to a stop in Trinidad off the coast of Venezuela in the south Caribbean. They then flew to Ascension Island in the South Atlantic, which is about a thousand miles from the west coast of Africa. Next stop was the Congo.

Chapter Eight

Covert Cuban Patriots

Once the C-124s landed in Albertville to off-load the pieces of the Swift Boats, a flurry of action began. Broussard writes in his diary that they hooked the cabin portion of the ship onto a truck and dragged it off the plane with ease. "It took one hour and forty-five minutes to unload the first plane," he says. A winch inside the giant Globemaster was attached to the small half of the hull and lifted high enough to install wheels underneath, and the hull was rolled out.

There was a narrow-gauge railway that ran along the edge of the runway to the Port of Albertville, and it played a significant role in our operations. As the parts were off-loaded onto Congo soil, they exited the plane on skids manufactured specifically to accommodate the plane's interior. Large tow trucks then dragged the skids to the rail line and the parts were hoisted piece by piece and placed on flatbed rail cars.

We transported the *Monty* and *Gitana* like colossal tinker toys, maneuvering the individual hulls and cabins down to the port where the Cajun experts would reassemble them. They were prepared to get the job done in a hurry, reconstructing the Swifts in just under three weeks.

Joe Bresch, an exceptionally skilled engineman and a part of Hamilton's team, came along with the Cajun builders. Bresch made sure that the engines were correctly reinstalled, that they operated perfectly, and that our crews had what they needed to maintain the engines properly to keep them in good running order. There were a few others in this group of specialist boat-technicians who made certain that the Swifts were shipshape in the end, and seaworthy for the mercenary Navy. Another old Frog, Bill Bain, was included on the team simply because he could do anything. Bain was like our leading utility player.

Back in the states, Tom Clines was assembling crews for the Swifts and would call on the trusted Cubans from the MRR.

But before Clines had a chance to contact him, Chavez tried to volunteer to go to Vietnam. The recruiter told him he had no obligation to do so, because he was past a certain age. Only hours after that attempted enlistment, Chavez received a call from Clines who asked him, "If you wanted to go to Vietnam, why didn't you just tell me?" Clines said he could fix Chavez up with a special position where there were Communist Cubans fighting against the Americans. He said he could make certain that Chavez was in the fight directly against Castro's thugs.

Clines was recruiting fast but all the time trying to keep the true nature of the Congo mission well under wraps.

Word began to spread among the MRR community in Miami that the "Company" needed them for a new anti-communist mission.

Chavez gathered a few of his most trusted crew members and told them they had been asked by "the Company" (whom they also referred to as "our friends") to go to Vietnam. When Chavez and his crew arrived at the Miami airport for the trip to Vietnam, they instead found that they were all ticketed to New York. It was only then that they were told their true destination: the Congo. The fact that they went along anyway is a profound example of the trust the Cubans had in Tom Clines.

They had heard rumors circulating among the exile community in Miami that Communist Cubans were fighting alongside the Soviet-backed rebels in the Congo, information that no national intelligence organizations had at that time. And it was also openly whispered that Che Guevara was there, leading them. It was enough information for this crew to sign up and go. They were prepared to fight Communist Cubans anywhere in the world.

But for Roberto Pichardo the decision to go to Africa was a difficult one. Pichardo had been a member of Brigada 2506 and participated in the invasion of Cuba at Playa Giron (the Bay of Pigs). He had endured the two-day assault expecting air cover or ground support that never arrived, and he was captured on April 23, 1961 off of the south coast of Cuba. He spent nearly two years in prison at Castillo de Principe, the Spanish fortress sited in Havana Bay overlooking the capital.

Through a negotiated exchange of prisoners for money and medicine, the Kennedy administration brought Pichardo and approximately 1,100 other Cuban-exile prisoners back to the States in December 1962. It was just two months after the end of the Cuban Missile Crisis. Pichardo arrived at the airport in Homestead, Florida on Christmas Day.

On December 29, in the Orange Bowl in Miami, Pichardo stood alongside other Cuban exiles who had been released and cheered with the rest when President Kennedy assured them that the flag of Brigada 2506 would one day be returned to them in a free Havana. He heard Mrs. Kennedy, in Spanish, express her hope that one day her son would grow up to be a man half as brave as the members of the 2506 Brigade.

Only days later, back in Miami, he was contacted by Luis Cosme, a fellow exile, who asked him to join a group that was going to Africa to fight communism. An air force of Cuban pilots was being recruited to fight in the Congo.

Roberto Pichardo had gone to Guatemala to train for the Bay of Pigs invasion in December 1960. He and his wife had one son, then nine months old, and another on the way. When he returned to Miami after the disastrous invasion and imprisonment, he had to tell Luis Cosme "no." "I just got back," he said. "I have two sons I don't even know. I want to be with my wife and boys."

Two years later he would finally make the trip to the Congo, but to be in the Cuban Congolese Navy, not the Cuban Air Force.

Once Clines had assembled the men he needed, the Cubans went in small groups of four or five at a time. Felix Toledo, who would be assigned to Chavez's boat crew, remembers waiting at the airport in New York to board the flight and wondering what was going to happen. He had no papers to travel internationally. The Castro Cubans had voided his passport. And upon arriving in the US the American immigration agents had simply torn that page marked "void" out of his passport. "You don't need that," he was told. He still has that passport.

The Pan Am flight out of JFK would land initially in Dakar, Senegal, and from there go on to Léopoldville in Congo. As the flight was announced, the small group of Cubans began to board, but the gate agents turned them away. Their lack of documents, or the insufficient documents they did hold, were not legal for travel.

Then, according to the Cubans, from out of the blue a "stranger" approached. A man that none of them knew or recognized, who was wearing sunglasses, spoke at length "in secret" to the gate agents, until finally the Cubans were waved ahead and allowed to board. They were the last ones on the plane and were ushered by a flight attendant to seats all the way at the back of the cabin. They were told to stay there and not get off the plane on the other end of the flight until everyone else was gone.

They had no idea who the "stranger" was, but had a pretty clear notion of whom he worked for.

Once they arrived in Léopoldville, they boarded Johnson's WIGMO flight to Albertville. When they arrived there, I stood alongside the Makasi pilots, who were flying missions for the Congolese Air Force, and waited as the Cubans got off the plane. I was anxious to honor Clines's turnover instructions.

Bill Hamilton and I eventually took charge of the Cuban crews and put them up at the Hotel Du Lac, but not for long. Chavez was interested in maintaining strict discipline among his crews and it was decided to rent them a house. "The Friends" purchased a used Volkswagen bus from a fleeing Belgian to transport the Cuban boat crews back and forth from the dock to the house. There would be no late-night drinking, no fraternizing with the mercenaries, and they were ordered to keep an extremely low profile.

Since the *Monty* and the *Gitana* were "their boats," and they knew the craft well, their assistance in reassembling the Swifts was invaluable. They played a significant role in the reconstruction and in assuring the seaworthiness and combat readiness of the boats.

Accustomed to onerous working conditions and motivated as they were, the Cubans pitched in alongside the Cajuns to get the boats ready in just over two weeks—an extraordinary achievement in those harsh conditions with limited resources.

Broussard, our lead Cajun, had a crew of five. The Cubans would arrive in stages, and Generoso Bringas and Papo Reyes were the first ones of our Cuban crew to get there and work with the Cajuns on reconstructing the Swifts.

The work began immediately. The first boat was unloaded and already under reconstruction when the second plane arrived the following day. The third plane, with critical parts on board, didn't arrive until five days later. This plane carried the smaller half of the hull and the superstructure. It never took longer than two hours to unload any one plane. And eight days after the first plane landed, the Cajuns had enough material to begin assembling the pieces of the hulls. By the end of day six, the Cajuns had the entire hull bolted together including the bow and cabin.

After they completed the first boat, Broussard notes in his diary that on the following day, "we are all jumping on the second boat," and began rigging and outfitting that Swift.

Broussard was a man of generous spirit, which is reflected in his feelings about the other Cajuns who volunteered for the assignment. He writes, "Tony (his right-hand man, Tony Dugas) has shown great ability for leadership. I couldn't have picked a better man—and that goes for the whole crew. I don't think I could have brought anybody to do more work than they done in the last seven days. They all deserve a pat on the back."

But he also makes a note of his one regret, that they didn't bring a carpenter. "The thing that gave us the most trouble on both boats is the carp work." But even with the lack of a qualified carpenter, they managed to accomplish a remarkable piece of work in a short amount of time.

When interviewed for this book, Broussard talked about the job he and his crew did. The CIA had apparently expected the reconstruction would take them two or three months to complete. He and his team did it in a month. He said, "I'm gonna brag: we were expert at this stuff, we built them from the keel up. I worked on the boats when I first went to Sewart and we knew every piece of the boat, we knew what we were foolin' with."

The Cajuns were slipped into the country undetected, "black in, black out" in the vernacular of the CIA. They were extremely hard-working and fun to be around, and looked at their efforts as a patriotic contribution. None of them was obligated to be there; they all went as volunteers. And there was no complaining or grumbling. They just worked from dawn to dusk, and had a cold Simba beer and a laugh at the end of the day. That's how I remember them the best. They were at it around the clock to reconstruct the fleet in the humidity and glaring sun, conditions that were familiar to the Louisiana natives.

And when the work was finished, they all boarded a commercial flight just like tourists and flew back home to Louisiana. Just one day after our Cajun boat builders completed the final rigging on the second Swift, the boats were on the water.

The rest of the Cuban crew then began to arrive. Ricardo Chavez, who would lead the men, arrived and was the one who made sure they kept their distance from the mercenaries in any social setting.

Roberto Pichardo gave the Swifts their new call signs once they were back on the water. The *Monty* was now "Lobo-1" and the *Gitana* would be "Lobo 2."

During the process of stitching the vessels back together, I remember a Belgian general and a British Army colonel had come through Albertville, and we gave them a tour of our works in progress. As the General toured the boat yard and inspected what was going on, he turned to me with a stunned look. "I can't believe my eyes," he said. He was completely dazzled by what he saw. I remember that the British colonel just shook his head in disbelief. "These Americans," was all he said.

I knew at that point that we were accomplishing something extraordinary.

Chapter Nine

Personal Differences

These events were a part of my bigger brief. I'd been given the authority to interdict supplies, weapons, and reinforcements, and eventually our objective would be to drive the Simba Rebels out of business. The spring and summer campaign had left the rebel's stronghold in Fizi battered but not broken, and the situation remained volatile.

Throughout the summer of 1965 the political situation in the Congo inexorably deteriorated. Telegrams and confidential memos were repeatedly exchanged between Washington and the embassy in Léopoldville. There was a growing feeling that the CIA's actions alone would not stop the expanding rebel insurgency. No intelligence-gathering capabilities existed within the Congolese government and consequently the CIA was asked to take up that role, a task that would absorb much of their funds and assets designated for the Congo.

In a December 1964 memo, DCI John A. McCone refers to the situation in the Congo as a "dreary" one. And here he states that the CIA should find ways to "interdict . . . rebel supplies." Our "MarOps," or maritime operations, were strictly CIA-run ventures and separately funded. Consequently, it was decided that my efforts to build and train the Navy were going to receive some additional help.

The Swifts were powered by high-performance Detroit Diesel GM V-1271 engines that were extremely reliable, as were the inboard/outboard gasoline engines on the little PTs, but maintenance and repair requirements were inevitable. Locally, the capabilities to perform that kind of work just didn't exist. Bill Hamilton naturally looked to the Teams for support, and he knew the right person for the job: Rene Gough, known as "Gooch."

When Hamilton was Commander of Underwater Demolition Unit-2

("Com UDU-2") at the Naval Amphibious Base in Little Creek, Virginia, Gooch served as a Frogman, with a specialty as an engineman. He stayed in that post until his retirement, when he left Virginia Beach and headed for an idyllic Caribbean spot in St. Thomas with his wife and four children. They had all sailed down to the Caribbean on a fifty-seven-foot retired oyster boat, a type of vessel known as a Chesapeake Bay Skipjack, which he had converted into a floating family residence. They had endured hurricane-force winds, a rejected landing sanctuary in Haiti by Papa Doc Duvalier's paranoid regime, and the impasse of the doldrums in the Sargasso Sea before pitching up for a couple of years on an idyllic island living aboard his sailboat, fishing, and enjoying being a family again.

Then the CIA came calling about a one-of-a-kind mission in the Congo. Ever the dedicated Frogman, Gooch could not say "no" to his old commander. This veteran "old Frog" would provide age and experience, because at twenty-six I was decidedly short on both.

He was the kind of guy who could do anything. A good sailor, a brilliant engineman, and a confidant and selfless friend. Gooch had the perfect demeanor for the job and when he arrived in the Congo he made an immediate impact on the smooth running of our operations.

The Cuban crew had difficulty pronouncing "Gooch," so they eventually distilled the name down to Bru. When he arrived, I presented him to the crew as the person who would be in charge of the maintenance on the boats. Roberto Pichardo remembers that he had the impression that Gooch was skeptical about their skills on the boats. The Cuban members of the crew were all very young, twenty-four or twenty-five, so I think Gooch naturally had doubts at first about whether they had enough experience or training.

Gooch also worked closely with the mercenary crews and properly trained them to perform routine maintenance. But in his downtime, he remained aloof from their nefarious activities, including their drunken brawls and their corruption. Because we worked with no true chain of command that would allow us to issue orders, our "command" had to be a combination of knowledge, competence, and bluff. Gooch was a natural at all of these.

Gooch and I took the same approach to the mercenaries. Soon after my arrival, aboard the *Kivu*, our Navy barracks ship, I had my one and only drinking session with them. I faked most of my alcohol consumption, making sure to keep my wits. It occurred to me very quickly that maintaining a clear head around the mercenaries was a necessity. I never drank with them again under any circumstances. I wanted to avoid familiarity with them, and beyond that, there was another much more serious element: the ubiquitous presence of weapons and the mercenaries' propensity to use them. Gather a bunch of drunken, heavily armed amateurs in a dingy backwater bar and you're not only looking for trouble, it's looking for you.

The Cuban training cadre also stayed clear of the mercenaries, at least socially. Chavez and I were in complete accord about this and knew it was best for everyone. They particularly gave a wide berth to the army troops, the ones who weren't a part of our navy. Yet sometimes these feelings nearly put the whole operation in jeopardy.

One evening in late October, Felix Toledo and Chavez stopped into the bar at the Hotel Du Lac to use the restroom. Felix made his way down the narrow hallway and encountered two exceptionally drunk 5 Commando soldiers. "Most of the time we tried to be polite," Toledo remembers. "But they were at the Hotel Du Lac because they were drunk, having fun. And something that they noticed is that we stuck together and didn't party with them."

Toledo recalls that they insisted he and Ricardo have a drink with them, to show their solidarity. Toledo turned on them. "With my face I was telling them to go to hell, and I said to them, 'I don't drink.'"

Chavez immediately recognized a potentially bad situation and quickly hustled Toledo outside. They made their way back to the van and Chavez instructed Toledo to "ratchet it down." He knew the mercenaries were dangerous and capable of gratuitous violence, and he needed Toledo to understand that, because they were vastly outnumbered, if he wasn't careful they might cut his throat. That would have been trouble we didn't need.

I recognized that among the Cubans there was a belief that they were fundamentally different from the mercenaries. They thought of themselves as a professional military force operating within certain moral and ethical lines. They saw no such boundaries among the mercenaries. "We were a military unit, but based ideologically in the same project," says Toledo.

The main distinction between the two groups was ideology. Where the

South Africans and Rhodesians fought for money and whatever loot they could pilfer, the Cubans fought for a cause. They were staunchly anti-Communist since the days of Fidel's takeover of their homeland, and they were paid modestly for their services. They weren't in the Congo to get rich and they didn't necessarily believe that the fighting there was going to get them their country back. But they felt as though it was a step, and that they were doing something to combat Communism.

The Cubans also felt they had a reputation to maintain. 5 Commando soldiers acted like they had a right to whatever they could steal, and that they were entitled to anything: the money in the local banks, the gold reserves transported from the mines on the national railroad, even personal valuables left behind in the homes where foreign residents fled the rebels.

When I had first learned that Cubans would be coming in to train the 5 Commando mercenaries, I realized there might be a potential problem. The mercenaries had a range of motivations for being in the Congo. Some were there strictly for the money, being paid for professional soldiering. But others were so perverted and deranged that they were there just because they "wanted to kill Kaffirs," the pejorative South African term for blacks. Fighting in the Congo conflict enabled them to do this and get paid for it. Because some of the Cubans were dark complexioned, I needed to make sure that before they arrived, they would be allowed to have a smooth introduction into the equation.

I approached Jock Cassidy. "Jock, these Cubans are professionals. They've been fighting a real adversary, not a bunch of ganja hyped-up teenage soldiers, and they know what they're doing." After allowing Cassidy to acknowledge this, I proceeded: "And some of the Cubans have dark complexions. So I'm holding you responsible, there better not be any trouble." Cassidy's reply was filled with perfect mercenary rationale. "No problem, Commander. They ain't Kaffirs, they're Cubans." And so our operation rolled on, fueled by a commitment to racial harmony.

The main challenge for the Cubans was to work on the Swifts and the PTs, trying to turn the 5 Commando personnel into sailors. Their task was to make the mercenaries capable of manning, maintaining, and operating the boats in a manner that would advance the interdiction mission and help put an end to the rebel insurgency. That was our focus.

In his first entry in the ship's log from the *Monty*, Ricardo Chavez states that the ship is "ready for navigating at Lake Tanganyika."

The first patrol took place thirteen days later and was a short-lived event. The crew set off at 5:40 in the evening and was back in port an hour later. The radar system malfunctioned and had no picture, so I radioed instructions for them to return to home base to get it repaired. The work was done quickly, because at 10:30 the next morning Lobo-1 set off again.

Interdiction operations were the purpose of the Force Navale Congolaise, so the Cubans, with the patience of saints, had to start from scratch training the 5 Commando recruits. I mean it was really down to basics. "Left side port; right side starboard, front is the bow, back is the stern." They had to be schooled to use the radar to vector the smaller craft and to distinguish actual potential targets from sea clutter.

Their training missions incorporated navigation, fluidity with the compass, relative and absolute, as well as strict radio communications procedures. They also had to be taught the lingo. "Roger" means "understood," "over" means "I am finished, you can speak," "wilco" means "will comply," and "out" means "the conversation is over." They may have thought they'd heard something like it in the movies, some over-coached actor saying "roger, wilco, over and out." But these expressions are used for a reason: they prevent misunderstandings through sloppy communications procedures. The last thing we needed in a covert war on a 418-mile-long, pitch-black lake was a miscommunication between the boats.

Correct use of the appropriate expression takes practice, and the mercenaries had little or no knowledge of this jargon. We had to make sure they got it right, and the Cuban team, professional and focused, worked diligently with the 5 Commando sailors to make certain that we could meet our objective.

The Cuban team worked hard to get the 5 Commando sailors seaworthy and weapons-ready. Although they had weapons training, most did not have experience firing with control and discipline.

Each Swift had .50 caliber machine guns mounted amidship, both port and starboard, plus one aft. The barrel above the cabin was also a firing position for the shoulder-fired .57mm recoilless rifle.

A useful gunfire support technique, acquired in Vietnam on the Swifts, was the employment of a .60mm mortar from the fantail. This was a kind of Rube Goldberg and "grab-ass" solution to create illumination on what would otherwise be an impossible platform for the purpose. Two sandbags and a board became the foundation on which the mortars could be fired to augment the gunfire capability. Accuracy was not the main purpose of illumination. At night, rather than shoot every moving vessel on the lake, illumination helped distinguish friend from foe and reduce innocent casualties by helping to ensure accurate fire at appropriate targets.

The 5 Commando sailors also needed instruction in the discipline of navigation. It was unlikely that the boats would get lost on the lake because it was sufficiently narrow and the shore was never far away. However, much of that shoreline was in hostile hands and the sailors had to learn to identify landmarks on the shore.

The radar could allow the navigator or helmsman to know the vessel's position in case it became necessary to beach for any reason, or to signal other FNC vessels the boat's exact location. Both of the Swifts and the *Ermans* had this capability, and the *Ermans* could then vector the Seacrafts.

Patrolling systematically in this way allowed for maximum coverage. The Cubans taught the mercenaries to keep accurate charts and logs of the patrol, to identify positions where contact had been made in order to establish rebel trans-lake patterns. It was a big task, but the Cubans had to incorporate all of these controls as part of the training curriculum.

One morning Roberto was having breakfast with Gooch at the Hotel Du Lac when word came that Lobo-2 had returned to port because of problems with the radar. Roberto and Gooch went down to the quay to check it out. After a brief investigation, Gooch returned to the hotel to finish breakfast, saying he'd be back in a little while to fix the radar. Roberto stayed behind to take a look.

He had installed the radar on the both Lobo-1 (then the *Monty*) and Lobo-2 (then the *Gitana*) back in Costa Rica. The systems had been handed to him in pieces, and he had to assemble and mount them, and consequently knew every nuance of that radar. They were Decca 202s and he had installed them piece by piece and under pressure. They were always short on time in Costa Rica while chasing Castro's navy, so a rapid and efficient assembly of the radar had been an overnight task for Roberto. Now, in Albertville, he discovered the problem right away.

Roberto Pichardo had been building radios since boyhood, a ham radio operator since the age of thirteen, which gave him a good knowledge of wiring. What he found on the Lobo-2's radar disturbed him. The wiring bore all the signs of having been intentionally cut. There was no way to know who might have done it or why. But Roberto was certain that it was not rats chewing through the wires, as some speculated. Someone who had access to the Swifts—and that was a limited number of personnel—could have gotten aboard and cut the wires.

Roberto had no way of proving that, nor any solid reason why it might have been done, except the always possible act of sabotage in a war zone where everyone would be looking to take any advantage possible. In that situation, everyone's loyalty was for sale.

Since it was an obvious problem, the repair only took him a few minutes to complete. He was quickly back at the hotel to let Gooch know that he'd found the problem and fixed it.

But Gooch had a hard time believing Roberto had accomplished the job in that short time. He returned to the dock to take a look for himself. When he examined the repair work, Gooch took an admiring glance and told Roberto, "I don't have to supervise you anymore; you know what you're doing."

Gooch's presence was a benefit to all of us. The Cubans relied on his wisdom and knowledge every day, and because of that we had dependable engines, and with him and Pichardo working closely together, we were ensured steadily functioning electronics. The working relationship between the Cubans and Gooch was seamless, and the Navy we built had come together with the *Ermans*, our Mothership, as the cornerstone of operations, the *Kivu* as our floating barracks, and the PTs and Swifts as the workhorses.

With the addition of Gooch to our team we were now becoming a real navy. The Swifts were pieced back together and operating effectively. Lake Tanganyika, the immense artery of rebel supply transport, was becoming our domain.

The Cubans executed regular patrols and the mercenary sailors were starting to shape up.

Chavez took a patrol out several times a week. They would be out for two or three days at a time and the *Monty* and *Gitana* (now Lobo-1 and Lobo-2) never went out on patrol together. They would go separately to maintain a rapid response in case anything happened to one of the boats.

Chavez's crew was consistent, including Felix Toledo and five others. Roberto Pichardo was at the base, in charge of communications. Our coded system ensured that nothing the enemy monitored could be deciphered. Sometimes they broke code, but mostly the Cubans maintained a good protocol and passed that ethic onto the mercenary sailors they were training.

This professionalism and discipline was clear early on during patrols that involved civilians, a sticky situation for any operator. On several occasions, the crew of Lobo-1 attacked boats on the lake that had women and children aboard. If they believed the men were enemy combatants, they would take prisoners aboard and either bring them back to base or make a rendezvous with the *Ermans*, the Mothership, until the prisoners could be delivered to 5 Commando in Albertville.

On December 30, Chavez reported coming across a boat on the lake. They maneuvered Lobo-1 in a circle around the small boat to take advantage of the moon to illuminate it. The ship's log notes that it was a boat with an outboard motor, a definite sign of a rebel vessel. Chavez ordered a high firing and immediately the boat attempted to get away.

Lobo-1 went into pursuit and instead of firing over their heads, the crew then took aim for real, firing several rounds. They approached the boat slowly and found that everyone on board had jumped into the lake and was trying to swim away.

Chavez ordered a slow speed chase, dogging the rebels through the water until they tired out. Lobo-1's crew fired a few rounds into the water, just to scare the swimmers, as Chavez recorded. They finally captured the rebels and brought them on board.

The Cubans were motivated by a general hatred of communism, but they also perceived early on in their recruiting that something was happening in the Congo that related to their Cuban problem. They would soon find out for certain. Rumors circulated throughout Miami that Communist Cubans were fighting in the Congo, but no one knew for sure if that was true or not. Until my Navy crew confirmed it.

It was a few weeks into these patrols that suspicions began to grow about the enemy on the other side. It was on a midnight patrol that Lobo-1 passed by the mountains along the banks of Lake Tanganyika and their radios began to pick up chatter. Toledo was on communications and he heard the enemy radio coming to life. "Tap tap tap," Toledo described the sound as it seemed to ring off the mountains, so clear, and so loud on the radio he thought it would break his eardrums.

Over that air he recognized something too familiar. The voices, the accents, the names: Lleyo, or Tico, he heard them calling each other openly by name. "Cubans are the same, doesn't matter what side you're on," he says. "We are still Cubans." Toledo went immediately to Chavez and said, "I know for certain, there are Cubans out there."

Chavez came back from that patrol and reported to me that he and the crew had detected and confirmed Cuban fighters on the other side. Chavez told me they could hear the communist Cuban soldiers complaining about the negative attitude of the rebels.

I contacted Johnson at the embassy to check on this, hoping he would verify it, but I was sure my crew had it right. It was late summer and I was expecting this wouldn't be new news to the staff at the embassy and particularly back at Agency Headquarters. Astonishingly, we were delivering information that no one back in DC had.

State Department documentation released in 2014 bears this out. There is not even a mention of Cuban communists until very late. A memo dated September 29, 1965, lays out the situation. Peter Jessup of the National Security staff writes to President Johnson that the "outlying areas remain chaotic and filled with marauding bands." He tells the president that the Fizi Baraka area has "given grave concern to the State Department. These rebels are being supplied across Lake Tanganyika by Russians and/or Chinese, and the rebel units are well armed and undergoing extensive training by Cuban guerrillas."

He goes on to inform Johnson that "the CIA has made a beginning in interdicting this support by the establishment of several boats based in Albertville to harass this supply route."

Our Navy was well documented in the State Department papers, but the existence of our Cuban-exile training cadre remained officially vague. In that same memo to President Johnson the mention of our Cuban-exile crew is deleted. It reads: "The only available nucleus of reliable covert boat operators is presently [*less than one line not declassified*]. It is planned to eventually replace them with Europeans. Mercenary adventurers and various Congolese tried thus far have proved disastrous as to discipline and ability to carry out their missions, to say nothing of maintaining the equipment."

Washington knew we were getting the job done, indicated in Jessup's note from the same memo: "Thus far, the pocket fleet has forced the rebels and their supporters to operate at night. The addition of radar to the new boats will make rebel runs more difficult." But there was reluctance by the US government to acknowledge that Cuban exiles staffed and trained the Force Navale Congolaise, despite numerous public media references to and photos of their involvement in the conflict.

About this time, as the Navy began to enter more vigorously into the fight, Headquarters determined that we needed a Chief of Base (COB). With both the air operations (AirOps) and our MarOps, plus the requirement for intelligence collection and reporting, they wanted us to have an experienced case officer to serve as COB. Ted Dern arrived about midsummer. He would offer us a textbook example of why fraternizing with the mercenaries was a hazardous proposition.

It appeared as though he was well suited for the assignment. He had worked in Laos and was fluent in French, which was the only common language in the Congo.

In the absence of an officer with Dern's qualifications, I had been "acting COB." But my three-week OpsFam course in Arizona was my sole knowledge of the Agency, and I had my hands full running the Navy. With the interdiction ops now ongoing, I was supervising the mercenary training by the Cubans, and LCol Hoare and I held daily strategy meetings to plan the missions in support of his ground troops. Consequently, Headquarters astutely wanted to have an experienced case officer as COB in Albertville.

Where Gooch and I steered clear of any after-hours bar time with the mercenaries, Dern took a different approach. His taste for alcohol regularly drove him to the mercenaries' favorite Albertville watering hole, and the frequency with which they drank and hung out together was enough to make me more

Jim in Vietnam/Military Assistance Command/Special Operations Group/Naval Advisory Detachment.

Jim and Gooch. Classic example of everything the term "swim buddies" encompasses.

Hawes and Tasos Maillis, owner of Greek fishing fleet and lake intelligence network.

Hawes and Ricardo Chavez, chief of the anti-Castro Cuban Congo Navy.

Force Naval's Congolaise mercenary Navy.

Crews of both Lobo-1 and Lobo-II, Cuban Congo Navy, plus Hawes (top left). Chavez seated third from left. Roberto Pichardo kneeling second from right.

Regimental Seargant Major 5 Commando, Captain of Force Navale Congolaise, Sam "Jock" Cassidy.

C-124 Globemaster disgorging one of the GM-1271 diesel engines from the Swift Boats destined for the Force Navale Congolaise interdiction fleet.

Our home in Albertville, the Hotel Du Lac. Some of our crew sitting out front after a long day.

Albertville, Main Street scene in front of Hotel Du Lac.

The port of Albertville, 1965. Operating base warehouse in the foreground.

Fleet of FNC—PTs, Swifts, *Ermans* (stern on dock for "high-tech" repair to propeller).

Lobo-1 underway, Ricardo Chavez commanding.

Lobo-2, plus the bow of *Ermans* on the right.

Crew of Lobo-1, over two Seacraft; Lobo-1 and the *Kivu*, our Navy barracks/mess ship in background.

Hawes (L), Chavez, Pichardo (R) at the 50th Reunion and Commemoration of the Stanleyville Hostage Rescue.

than uncomfortable. I give him the benefit of the doubt here, because perhaps he felt there was some intelligence-collection advantage to spending so much off-duty time with the mercenaries.

But that socializing with the mercenaries would nearly cost him his life and potentially destroy the Navy.

Chapter Ten

Wrapped Around a Bottle

It was well after midnight when there was a loud banging on my hotel room door. Even though half asleep, I instinctively picked up my Walther PPK from the night table and went reluctantly to the door. It's never good news at that hour. I eased the door open slowly. A severely inebriated Jock Cassidy stood swaying in the hallway. Behind him the tall, gangly Dern was quaking with fear. The color had drained from his face and he was so pale with fright that he almost seemed to glow in the dark.

I shook my head at the sight of them, and Cassidy immediately blurted out, "Commander, this arsehole insulted me in front of the men." I thought about Cassidy's foul temper, and having witnessed his vengeful brand of discipline with the "go-fer" he had tormented over the food-stealing incident. I knew he was capable of meting out irrational punishment.

Cassidy glared at Dern. "I am going to kill him," he said. His eyes flared with an alarming rage that continued to build. "And then I'm gonna burn down the Navy."

Dawn was still several hours in front of us, so a clear light-of-day solution didn't seem an immediate option for Cassidy's threat. Jock Cassidy meant what he said. His volatility was becoming more evident to me the longer we worked together, despite how well we were progressing in the development of the Navy.

I stepped back into my hotel room and held the door open a little wider. As Cassidy started to enter, I motioned to Dern to stand fast. I needed to diffuse the tension and to do it quickly, before Dern did something really stupid. My instincts told me that I needed to maintain a casual atmosphere in this situation.

"Come on in," I said. "Tell me what happened and let's talk about it."

Cassidy stepped into my room and I immediately turned to Dern and jabbed my finger in the direction down the hall toward his room, signaling him to get the hell out of there. Now. He stumbled away with an uneven gait, the dead giveaway of the intoxicated. I closed the door and motioned for Cassidy to sit down.

The room was small so there wasn't much distance between us. He had a weapon strapped to his side and he fingered the trigger and barrel continuously. I kept an attentive eye on him, not because I thought he had any hostility toward me but because of his unpredictability.

After several tense moments Cassidy repeated his threat, "Commander, I'm going to kill him. He insulted me in front of the men. I'm going to kill him and then I am going to burn down the Navy."

My first instinct was to switch Cassidy's focus to try and control the conversation. I replied, "Jock, I don't give a shit if you kill Dern. Go ahead. But why would you want to burn down the Navy? We've worked so hard to build it!"

That tactic succeeded almost immediately in shifting Cassidy's concentration from Dern to the Navy, and was enough to lower his intensity.

Then I received an earful from this wild-eyed Scotsman and I listened until dawn, shaking my head in sympathy at the appropriate moments and subtly admonishing him when the timing seemed right, taking every opening to applaud our mutual efforts in developing the Navy.

Cassidy's criteria for "punishment by death" came from an argument that had started in the mercenaries' watering hole. It was a typical drunken mercenary foray, one misunderstood comment lobbed on top of another until all parties were irrationally insulted, and furious enough to draw guns to try and prove their manhood.

But Cassidy's emotional makeup didn't allow him to simply reconsider the perceived insult that Dern had made. In his mind, Cassidy felt that Dern had insulted him in front of "his" mercenaries, the very ones Cassidy had trained, the ones in whom he'd calculatedly instilled a dose of fear. His exaggerated pride could not allow this perceived outrage to go unpunished. And there was no changing his mind or letting it pass. As far as he was concerned the gauntlet had been thrown and the only response was that Dern should die.

What baffled me was why Cassidy dragged Dern to my door that night instead of just killing him outright. Could it be that deep down, Cassidy wanted to be talked out of this murderous event? But even in retrospect this notion seems unlikely. Perhaps he felt that we'd formed a bond of respect, and he was demonstrating that here, in a peculiar Cassidy kind of way. I know that I was the only officer who had kept my word to him consistently and who had dealt with him in a professional manner. Maybe this was his response to some unique regimental discipline in his life. The real answer will never be known.

Cassidy had lived most of his adult life under these uncivil circumstances. Operating in a lawless atmosphere, adhering to a barbarous code that didn't require reason or patience or judgment. When he was befuddled by booze, he might best be described as trigger-happy. I knew there needed to be a delicate balance between placating him and just accepting his ruthless thuggery outright. In his twisted logic, burning down the Navy was the natural extension of his anger at Dern. And Dern ending up dead here was the most worrying part of the equation.

As Chief of Base, Dern was as entitled to protection as any Agency officer. I had seen enough, however, to know that he hardly lived up to the caliber of an official I wanted to defend. But if Cassidy's displaced anger could actually put our mission in jeopardy by killing the COB, I needed a plan to deal with it, and couldn't allow it to just boil over until it was too late.

In the sobering dawn, Cassidy relented to a certain degree and the sunrise finally turned his attention to sleep.

After hours of contradictory declarations about how he'd go about burning down our Navy, then paradoxically acknowledging our accomplishments with pride, he started to soften. But he was absolutely adamant on one point that I had offered as a way to get him to back off his intent. I would keep Dern away from him and from any part of the Navy and crews. And in exchange for that pledge, the Force Navale Congolaise would operate at an increased tempo. With a mood swing worthy of a classic manic-depressive, he began an enthusiastic outline of a couple of our upcoming missions.

I assured Cassidy that I would keep Dern far out of his sight and then I sent him back to the *Kivu* to sleep off the remaining bad blood. I watched him march down the hall and heard him thunder down the stairs, taking them two at a time. Even a long, drunken night didn't dent his capacity for self-possession. Hard-shelled, psychotic, murderous. I needed to hatch a backup plan for keeping Dern alive and Cassidy under control.

As soon as he was gone I went immediately down to Dern's room for the follow-up. I banged on his door loudly. I didn't care if he'd only had a few hours' sleep, I was going to have it out with him.

But I was wrong. After an over-intoxicated bar incident that nearly got him killed, he didn't go to bed to sleep it off. He continued drinking. He sat alone in his room wrapped around a bottle for nearly five hours. The all-too-real fear that Cassidy would follow through on his threat had hammered away at him through the better part of a fifth of scotch. Now he sat trembling, whiter than the sheets on the bed.

I told him I thought Cassidy's threat was genuine, and that he would kill him without hesitation. I suggested maybe the best thing would be for Dern to be on the next available supply aircraft out of Albertville. He immediately agreed and decided that that was what he was going to do. He would make arrangements to leave as soon as possible.

But for the interim that he remained at our base, I had to figure out how to protect Dern, who was after all one of us, even if he was ill suited for this assignment. And protecting him would require action on Cassidy.

This presented its own set of difficulties. I couldn't just lock him up. It would mean indignity for Cassidy beyond calculation and a loss of the image of strength that was essential to all our well-being and to Cassidy's control of the mercenaries. And the worst possibility was that the mercenaries would seek to free Cassidy and it would be Gooch and me against all them.

I knew that at any moment, especially if he got drunk, that Cassidy was capable of flipping into an emotional rage regarding Dern and that would have disastrous results. I went to Gooch for counsel and advice and to work out a plan.

I asked him to come with me out to the end of the quay where no one could possibly eavesdrop on our conversation. We sat at the edge of the water looking across Lake Tanganyika. The wind was up and the swells were beating high against the pylons. "We have a big problem," I said. "It's Dern."

He turned to me and half rolled his eyes. "He's a pain in the ass," Gooch said. "Worse than that," I replied. "He shot off his mouth in the bar, somehow insulting Cassidy in front of a bunch of the 5 Commando. Now Cassidy thinks he has to kill Dern to preserve his honor."

Gooch considered this for a minute. "Sounds like the classic reaction. He needs to maintain his stature among the mercs, right?" I nodded.

"Dern deserves to be killed for being so stupid," I said. "But it's not really an option, is it?" Gooch and I looked at each other, then he chuckled. "Seems like our choices boil down to a few bad ones. Can't get Cassidy to calm down and back off his threat, correct?" I nodded. "We can remove Cassidy, but then we lose our captain and probably control of the men." Again, I agreed fully.

"What if you send Cassidy out on an extended patrol?" Gooch offered.

I considered this for a moment, but then rejected it out of practicality. "Cassidy never goes on patrol," I said. "He assigns the crews according to our original agreement. He controls the men. I control the operations."

Gooch nodded immediately. He understood exactly what that meant. If I told Cassidy to take out a patrol it would be counter to how we had always operated. After his years of working in this cutthroat business, constantly looking over his shoulder for the knife in the back, he'd be justifiably suspicious, and probably hostile. And it might provoke the very event we were trying to avoid.

The only sound for several minutes was that of the waves thumping against the dock. Then Gooch said, "We gotta get Dern out of town."

A squad of B-26Ks then made a pass overhead, the Makasi pilots coming in for a landing at the airstrip. The intense rumble of their engines as they made a banking turn and flew over us seemed to add a note of urgency to the conversation. I told Gooch, "I'm afraid there's only one way to make sure Cassidy doesn't execute his threat before we can get Dern on a plane." Gooch looked over at me. He had that knowing acknowledgment of how seriously exposed we'd be if Cassidy actually did kill Dern.

It was getting late in the day by this time and the sun was casting long shadows across the water, lighting up the boats tied alongside the quay. Our Navy, bobbing nearby on the choppy lake, was in crisis. Something drastic in the form of a backup plan had to be put in place to break the looming threat.

Cassidy's venom was too authentic to be ignored, and Gooch and I recognized this with a deep sense of accountability. We had to protect our own. That was our obligation. Cassidy had to be dealt with before he showed any attempt to move on Dern. We agreed that that required a serious plan of action, one that we would undertake only if it were absolutely necessary. It had to be a plan of elimination.

This could never be discussed with Léopoldville, of course. We wouldn't reveal it to anyone. No one would want to know about it on the assumption that knowledge would be tantamount to approval. And this couldn't be approved by anyone, and couldn't be known about by anyone not directly involved.

In those kinds of circumstances, under a lethal threat, we both understood what had to be done. Ours was a job that demanded cold, calculated, professional judgment. It was a local problem and could only be dealt with locally, not in a faculty lounge or embassy conference room. The morality of the plan boiled down to a "kill or allow to be killed" decision. We both knew Dern was not capable of protecting himself. And I believed that Cassidy was capable of murder.

After putting together several different scenarios for elimination, Gooch said glumly, "If we do this, there is always the possibility of revenge by one of the mercs." I replied, "Not we, Gooch. This is my responsibility. So, let's figure out how to do it in a way that gives me plausible deniability."

It was nearly dark at this point and we were walking off the dock back toward town. Gooch stopped and looked out at the lake again. It was now nothing but an obsidian canvas stretching from horizon to shore. He asked, "Can Cassidy swim?"

It was a natural question from an old Frog and right on point. I shook my head "no." And we decided then and there that our plan would be executed on the water. We would take advantage of my training and my abilities, and use them against Cassidy's weaknesses. I was a combat swimmer. Cassidy didn't swim at all. This uncomplicated difference in our skill sets brought Gooch and me to a simple, solidly results-oriented plan.

I would take Cassidy out on one of the small boats for a post-maintenance test of the motors. We'd sail into the middle of the lake, far from shore. I would be armed with a grenade and ready to swim. At the right moment, I would drop the grenade into the engine compartment and, in nearly the same motion, dive overboard. If the explosion didn't take out Cassidy, then he would drown.

A fumes-in-the-engine compartment boat accident would be a plausible explanation for his death. It was well known that venting of the engine space was essential to prevent just such an "accident." Dern would be protected and a bad deed would prevent another bad deed.

Fortunately, the resolution came much more easily and we never had to put that plan into action. Dern left Albertville on the next WIGMO flight that took off two days later. He had stayed in his room the entire forty-eight hours and therefore out of Cassidy's way, so he got out of town before events proceeded to a lethal conclusion for one or the other of them.

The head of my mercenary Navy, someone I knew to be an unhinged drunk and a plunderer, remained sober on the job and helped us execute a season full of successful patrols and raid support. But Gooch and I discovered in the end that we hadn't devised that plan simply out of melodrama.

The following year, Cassidy's hair-trigger temper would lead him directly back to an intoxicated confrontation, only this time the perceived insult resulted in an unarmed WIGMO contractor taking a Cassidy bullet directly in the face.

Chapter Eleven

Signs and Rumors of Che

After Dern's departure, our team shifted into a new gear. The Lobo-1 would stay in port while the Lobo-2 went out, and vice versa. The Cubans and mercenary crew ran the Swifts, the *Ermans,* and the PTs on interdiction raids almost on a nightly basis, and the ship's log reflects those engagements with enemy troops from as far north as Baraka all the way back down to our home base of Albertville, hundreds of miles at a stretch.

Our Navy, with our own well-traveled and reassembled Swifts, was operating in a different kind of war. It was still a global conflict but a covert one, made up of proxy wars between the democratic west and the communist east. It was not as simple as that, of course, but our Cold War mission in the Congo, to close down supply lines that had fueled Simba rebel activity, was about weakening insurgent capabilities, holding a line against communism, and protecting America's interests. The results of our raids were also beginning to bear unexpected fruit.

In the mid-1960s, Cold War politicking was turning into an art form. It's difficult now to imagine the atmosphere. Unlike any other time in history, two superpowers had the ability to completely obliterate life on our planet. And they came close. After the Cuban Missile Crisis, where the world had been tipped to the brink of a nuclear exchange, the fear of a Communist takeover didn't simply drive political anxiety, it mass-produced it. The US and the Soviets faced off in a punch and counter-punch policy of spying, intelligence gathering, and espionage that would last for another three decades and result in an ever-escalating buildup of nukes, a policy that would be termed MAD (mutually assured destruction.)

My time in the Congo occurred in the heart of this Cold War turmoil.

The numbers of weapons grew and their delivery systems became increasingly sophisticated. The techniques for spying on one another evolved and improved and the specter of a communist revolution that would "topple the dominoes" attracted one side and repelled the other. The collective preoccupation of that potential event drove every government and international spying organization to step up its game, by any means necessary.

Within this atmosphere there were rumors circulating in the media and in the intelligence traffic that Che Guevara, the future iconic face of communist revolution, was on the move. He had disappeared from public life in Cuba and had not been heard from, fueling speculation not only about his whereabouts, but also about his strained relationship with Fidel Castro.

Later, Castro read a letter Che had written in which he renounced his honorary Cuban citizenship and resigned his post as the Cuban Minister of Industry, a position too passive for a man of his passionate revolutionary zeal. It was assumed that Che's relentless desire to export the revolution would compel him look for his next battle. There had been reported sightings of him in Egypt and elsewhere in Africa, but these reports were usually unsubstantiated. There were rumors of his presence in Tanzania and Congo, but nothing that was reported could be confirmed.

It was known that Laurent Kabila, the leader of the Simbas, spent much of his time in Tanzania, and of course the Tanzanian lake port of Kigoma was the departure point for most of the weapons and supplies destined for Eastern Congo's Simba Rebels. And our Force Navale Congolaise was systematically disrupting their lake traffic by interdicting supplies, taking prisoners, and confiscating their weapons.

As time passed and rumors of Che's whereabouts persisted, Chavez and his crew would uncover a critical piece of that international puzzle while out on lake patrol one night.

The idiosyncrasies of Lake Tanganyika could create unusual conditions, such as collections of massive vegetation large enough to resemble small islands drifting in the lake. They sometimes even included trees that broke off of the banks when heavy rainfall flooded into the rivers that fed the lake. These large pieces of "land" could float with the current and be blown by the wind until they slowly disintegrated from the surface action of the water.

More than once the crews had been out on the lake and seen these floating islands on the radar and had mistaken them for boats.

Chavez and crew set out on Lobo-1 during a new moon on a dark, clear night. The lake was black and calm and they were about fifteen or twenty miles from port. Crew member Felix Toledo recalls that they observed something floating, which in the pitch black of night they assumed was another one of these "vegetation islands." But since they also knew that in very low visibility these formations could actually be boats, the crew continued to scrutinize the floating "vegetation." They identified what appeared to be five distinct pieces of debris on the water that were stuck together, further tweaking their curiosity.

At full alert, with weapons ready, they eased in closer. Suddenly, it was apparent that these "islands" were drifting in slightly different directions. The crew figured it out almost immediately. They weren't vegetation islands, but a covey of boats having a rendezvous on the lake.

I was back at base monitoring the radio and I suddenly heard Ricardo Chavez's voice shout, "Attack!"

The distinct *pop, pop, pop* of machine gun fire came crackling through the radio, immediately distinguishable from the mundane static and clutter. My ear was attuned to the prospect of a firefight and the hair on my arms began to prickle as that unmistakable sound cut through the feeble reception of our rudimentary equipment. The Swifts were out on the lake and in some shit. The only question was how deep.

The boat crew opened fire first with semi-automatic Soviet AK-47s, weapons we'd captured in previous raids. That was one of the ways we hurt them: using their own guns against them. If the boats got really close during the melee of the firefight, the AKs would come in handy.

Lobo-1 was armed for combat, carrying .50 cal machine guns mounted amidships, port, starboard, and aft, plus a shoulder-fired .57mm recoilless rifle on the gun tub above the cabin.

A concussive barrage erupted as five enemy vessels returned fire, bullets screaming between the boats. Toledo recalled the events vividly: "As soon as we made contact, one boat separated from the group. In hindsight, we realized it was obviously to distract us, leaving us to contend with the other four boats that were firing intensely."

The fifth boat that cut away was stationed a short distance behind the others, not firing a shot, just waiting, as if trying to decide whether to re-engage or depart.

Then, their decision made, the fifth boat suddenly swung around and opened up again in a hail of bullets that covered their escape as it sped east, across the black waters of Lake Tanganyika toward the enemy refuge of Tanzania.

I stood by the radio listening, my adrenaline surging. From my own experience on Swifts, the sound of the weapons told me that the boats were fencing, maneuvering for position to maximize their concentration of firepower.

Time seems to stand still in these intense encounters, especially in a night black as coal with only illumination from periodic tracers. After what seemed like hours, two enemy boats stopped returning fire and pulled away, leaving Lobo-1 to face the remaining pair. They were no match for the shelling our crew hurled at them. The final shots blew the boats apart. Chavez and the rest of the crew watched as they sank without a trace, casualties of superior, disciplined firepower from the crew of Lobo-1.

After the firefight, Chavez got on the radio to me at the base and I told them to report back. It was just after dawn when Lobo-1 pulled up to the quay. Even in the low morning light it was obvious they had seen action. The Swift was bullet-pocked, riddled with holes in the cabin and sides, and the weapons were still hot. The men looked drained and exhausted.

As a CIA contractor, I was strictly forbidden from participating in this combat—McKay had learned that the hard way in the assault on Fizi Baraka. If I were caught or killed, the revelation of direct US involvement in this covert operation could give away and potentially jeopardize the entire mission. I rarely breached that order, but when I did my team respected the need to never disclose it. They protected my butt from any bosses who were too remote to appreciate what had to be done is such circumstances. But it was on nights like this one, as a trained covert combatant, that I desperately wanted, and felt I needed, to be personally in the fight.

I debriefed Chavez and it was clear to both of us that there was something very curious about that fifth boat. The manner in which it had escaped suggested it sheltered someone or something important. A VIP, we thought—otherwise the remaining enemy boats would not have put up such a fierce resistance. Their previous behavior had consistently been "cut and run."

We had already discovered that Castro Cubans were fighting alongside the communist rebels. We had detected their radio calls, because they weren't even disciplined enough to protect names or language. They blatantly violated even minimal tactical cover over the radio. And of course, one Cuban recognizes another.

So who had been out on that boat? Who merited such fierce protection?

We believed it had to be Che Guevara. It was reasonable to assume that it would have taken someone of the stature and importance of Che to motivate the four boats to remain in the fight to sacrifice themselves in order to give the fifth boat, possibly containing a VIP in need of protection, the opening to withdraw and escape.

Those in the spook world who studied Che closely followed the reported sightings of him in countries sympathetic to the revolution. Intelligence traffic at CIA and NSA was flooded with information that marked Che's presence in any leftist-inclined country as a major indicator of instability and at risk of communist revolution. It was more than a matter of curiosity to the intelligence community, because it was felt that Che was a barometer for which country would emerge as the next threat of communist armed rebellion.

A couple of days later the intelligence we received from 5 Commando, which had seized a cache of documents, provided confirmation that there had been Cubans aboard that fifth boat that had escaped. It was a fact that finally validated what we had reported weeks earlier, that Cubans were fighting in Congo alongside the Simbas. Now there was no doubt; everybody knew. What wasn't confirmed was the very strong possibility that it was Che Guevara on board that boat that had escaped in the firefight. We believed it was. As Toledo says, "he slipped through our fingers." But we'd get another shot at him.

In Guevara's diary, *The African Dream: The Diaries of the Revolutionary War in the Congo*, he writes about the pressure he and the rebels felt from the 5 Commando ground troops and from our Navy's interdiction efforts. By our daily patrols, we had been able to nearly close down the rebel supply lines, which created a shortage of everything, particularly food. But we also made sure weapons, ammunition, and medicine could not reach their base.

They were systematically being deprived of everything they depended on as our Navy began to live up to its capabilities. The battle strategy was working exactly as we had planned and prepared for.

We intensified patrolling even more, and as Che's diary indicates, the intimidation factor we created kept the captains of their vessels from even attempting trans-lake supply missions. As supplies ran out, the attrition rate kicked up, and toward the end of summer the Simbas began deserting. Those desertion numbers would escalate slowly and then become a critical exodus into the fall campaign.

Our original Navy interdiction mission had been defined without regard for Che Guevara and his band. But the knowledge of his presence would be an adrenaline jolt for us. Our "point of the spear" operation now looked like a high priority for the communists, with implications far beyond our pay grades.

In response, the Agency would ante up, with accelerated delivery of vital spare parts, a single sideband radio to improve communications, and an experienced case officer who expanded our ability to collect and analyze intelligence. With beefed-up support, our Force Navale Congolaise went to all ahead, full. We weren't going to allow the enemy an upper hand, even if they felt they had a seasoned revolutionary commander leading them. We were determined to draw the battle lines. Our tactics would dictate strategy and be the game-changers, not the other way around.

Chapter Twelve

Threats from Every Direction

While the pace of our missions quickened and their success rate increased, a unique hazard of the Congo took a toll on me.

On a blustery October afternoon, I felt the first harbinger of a Congo peril. The sky was gray and clouds were thickening on the horizon, a perfect indicator that a storm was building, in more ways than one. From the pickup of the wind speed I knew that we were in for trouble. This was the first severe lake storm that I had experienced. It was a high sea state and at the time I didn't realize the depth of the problems the weather was brewing.

Tanganyika is the largest and deepest rift lake in Africa, created when tectonic plates began to shift within the continental crust. The lake is the second largest body of fresh water, by volume, in the world. Like many of these lakes, it is bound by steep cliffs along the fault margins and the configuration of those cliffs affect wind currents and velocity. With 1,136 miles of shoreline, it's 418 miles long and 45 miles across at its widest point. A strong storm gusting the hundreds of miles down the lake's corridor is squeezed along the channel created by the cliffs, and that turns the lake into a giant wind funnel. Sea states can reach six feet and more.

As the storm began to pick up that afternoon, my instinct told me I'd better get down to the port. I sprinted the half-mile to the quay where the Swifts were docked and found the waves building with an alarming size and frequency.

It was clear that the boats would soon be hammered against the quay, which could cause catastrophic damage to the hulls and framework. The storm developed so quickly that there were few Navy personnel to respond. Those that were present had never experienced anything like this and did not know what to do.

I boarded the outboard Swift, started the motor, and steered it several hundred yards from the quay, a safe distance away but still in the harbor area. I turned it over to one of my crew, who took the wheel and maneuvered the boat away to a safer position.

I stood on the Swift deck and looked back, then I pulled off my shoes. I realized that this member of the Navy crew was staring at me, a skeptical look on his face. He had just realized that I was about to dive into the water.

What he didn't understand is that for the SEALs our fallback position is always "go to the water." No other Special Forces conduct the extensive water training that SEALs do and it gives us a particularly useful edge on the enemy, because no one is more at home in rough water than we are. For me, on that day, it was the easiest, quickest, and safest operational mode of transport.

There was another boat thrashing against the quay and I didn't need to think twice about whether diving into a surging storm swell was the appropriate strategy. It was the best alternative to avoid any potential threat to our fleet.

I stripped off my shirt and dove in. The sea was extremely choppy and even that short swim was laborious. I was plowing through four- to six-foot swells of turbulent water and that can take your strength away pretty quickly. But I'd swum through a lot worse. In my training alone I'd been thrown into numerous rough seas under frigid conditions at the end of long days of exhausting maneuvers. This wasn't a holiday swim by any means, but my mindset and my physical capabilities were prepared to withstand the conditions.

I reached the quay and pulled myself out of the water quickly, hurried over to the inboard Swift, and climbed up.

By now the sea state had reached the point of being dangerous to the integrity of the boats, high enough to create a potentially catastrophic event. A massive wave could lift the boat over the quay and as the water receded, the action would bring the Swift crashing down. If that happened, the force would probably break the keel, which would mean severe damage that would be impossible to repair in that ill-equipped facility in Albertville. Salvaging the Swifts was imperative; our entire operation depended on it.

Just as I started the engines, a monster wave rose under the boat and we caught the crest. My worst fears were becoming a reality. The mammoth wave gained altitude and velocity as it blasted against the dock and tossed the boat over the quay. I was hanging onto that helm for dear life, white-knuckling the throttle as a ten-foot wave hoisted the boat up. I felt the surge and recognized that we were poised to drop back down on top of the quay, which would surely crush the Swift underneath me.

Action became a blur and once more instinct took over. As the wave reached its crest I immediately slammed the throttles into reverse, a backward thrust that jolted me like a bulldozer to the chest. That propulsion, coupled with the recession of the wave, drove the Swift back down into the water. I hit the throttles and shoved them forward and yanked hard starboard on the wheel. The boat spun, bucking like a young stallion. I got control quickly and steered the Swift away from the quay, engines whining at full speed.

I sailed the distance in the blinding rain, crossing the water to where the other Swift was parked. The crew members and I made both boats secure, lashing them down to be able to ride out the storm without being in any further danger.

In the middle of all this, with the intensity of the rain pelting down and the powerful waves thrashing the quay, I had a bizarre sensation that distracted me just momentarily. It was as though a convulsive chill surged through my body from somewhere deep inside. I dismissed it. I was sopping wet from the swim and shivering cold standing in the rain. The wind was at high velocity and felt like it was cutting right through me.

But the immediate tasks of saving the Swifts, the nuclei of the Navy, took precedence over everything else. I've thought back on that moment a few times and wondered how I might have reacted to that feeling if I had been anywhere else, like back in my hotel room. But at that moment when the first symptom hit me, my concentration was elsewhere, so I put the warning aside and continued to batten down and secure the rest of the fleet.

After the crisis passed and the storm started to recede, I returned to the Du Lac. Later that evening, down in the dining room, the shaking began. It was not a shiver but a convulsive, full-body rattle. A violent physical quaking that just wouldn't stop. I went up to my room, lay on the bed, and almost immediately became violently ill. From both ends. A boiling inferno of a fever began to spike up and down, and the brutal retching continued throughout night.

By the next morning the fever was constant and raging. Every joint in my body was on fire, screaming for relief. Any movement felt as though the joints were trying to bend in the wrong direction. For the next two days, sapped of my ability to do anything, including stand up, I lay in bed shackled to a vicious Congo fever. Any kind of nourishment was out of the question, because even just a sip of water was difficult to keep down.

There was nothing even remotely akin to medical resources in Albertville, but someone eventually brought a "doctor" to my room. I had no idea where he was from, but he was a swarthy Caucasian and I couldn't even discern what language he spoke. We were reduced to hand signals. He dug a couple of pills out of his bag and with pointing and gestures urged me to take them. I just shook my head. I didn't have much strength, but I had enough to say "no." If the fever wasn't going to kill me, I'd be damned if I'd swallow some mystery medication administered by a medical wannabe. I already had enough problems.

After several more days of unabated symptoms, our Morse operator became alarmed and told me that if I continued like that, he was afraid I might actually die. I don't think he wanted to be responsible for that. He sent a message to the station in Léopoldville telling them that I needed help, and soon, or I might not pull through.

The next day the WIGMO C-46 arrived on its regular logistics stop. Several of my crew helped me get to the airstrip, which included a nauseating car journey over the rough, potholed roads of Albertville. The crew helped me board the plane, where I was the sole passenger.

The all-day flight to Léopoldville, across the broad expanse of the Congo jungle, seemed endless. The pilot was one of the Makasi Cubans, who were rumored to not be trusting of or inclined to fly by instruments. Consequently, with no other navigational aids, it was a bouncy and twisting flight as the pilot picked his way through the air, passing over hostile areas that held the constant prospect of a lucky shot from the ground.

I sat alone in the back. The wracking fever had begun to subside some, but by this time I was sapped of strength from having nothing to eat and little water for the past several days. I was severely dehydrated and feeling light-headed enough without the jockeying through the air.

Four to five days had passed since the onset of the fever and I felt reassured now that I probably wasn't going to die. By the time the C-46 arrived in Léopoldville, I knew exactly what I needed, and badly: food and water. I was sure that would be the best medicine for me in order to beat this jungle disease.

As I exited the airplane that late afternoon I actually felt better. Dick Johnson was there to meet me and, being the great boss he was, he demonstrated care and attention to my needs. He told me I looked like shit.

Johnson could have sent someone of lower rank to pick me up, but he had a keen sense of leadership and was dedicated to the welfare of his Team. Concern was something he would never delegate. He expected to see me on a stretcher, I think. But instead, I bounded off the plane, feeling much better than when we'd taken off. What a difference eight hours could make after your body has fought off a mysterious jungle fever.

I said to Johnson, somewhat sheepishly, "Dick, I am embarrassed to say, I think I'm going to live." He steered me toward his waiting Land Rover as he said, "Maybe. But you're going to the hospital."

I checked into a former Belgian Hospital, Louvanian, which was the premier hospital in Léopoldville, now run by the Congolese. I was sent to a private room and waited. Absolutely nothing happened. No one came by to do any tests. No doctors showed up to listen to my lungs. No nurses with needles came to take my blood. No examinations or words of comfort, no thermometer shoved under my tongue, or anywhere else. But most importantly, no one brought me any food and I only received a small amount of water. I had overcome the fever, but I was now borderline frantic for some real food and large amounts to drink.

I put up with it for twenty-four hours. Then, after receiving no attention whatsoever, I became my own best medical advocate. I prescribed an exit directly to a hot meal. I got up, got dressed, and walked out of the hospital. No one seemed to care or even notice. I hailed a taxi, feeling like if I didn't get something to eat soon the fever hadn't killed me but starvation would. I asked the taxi driver to take me directly to a restaurant. The meal I finally devoured might be the single most satisfying food have I ever had. It wasn't fancy, but it was exactly what I needed and I savored every bite. I have never forgotten how gratifying it was.

After that I made my way to the embassy to report in to Johnson. He was a bit surprised to see me and wanted to know how my hospital stay had gone. I replied convincingly that everything seemed okay, and that whatever it was that had poisoned me seemed to finally be out of my system.

Johnson instructed me to stay around Léopoldville for a few days. He didn't want me returning to Albertville before he could be sure that I was fully recovered. He told me to go to a safe house and just rest for a couple more days.

That's almost what I did, but not exactly. I did go to the safe house. But I didn't do a lot of resting, because later that evening I met Gail. In terms of things I remember most strongly from my time in the Congo, Gail far surpasses even the meal I'd had. I'd been trapped in the claustrophobic village atmosphere of Albertville for several months, so spending the evening in a metropolitan city, out on the town in the anodyne company of a gorgeous female, was better medicine than I deserved.

Gail was an American serving in the USIS (United States Information Service) office in Léopoldville. She was from upstate New York and very bright with an adventurous streak, which was probably the winning combination that got her selected by the USIS to go to Congo as part of the US Embassy team. Congo was her first foreign assignment. It was luck coming together for me again that brought me into Léopoldville at that exact right moment in order to meet her. Gail was smart, adventurous, worldly, wonderful. She had shoulder-length auburn hair and blue eyes, stood about five foot six, and was also gifted with an athlete's body, trim and fit, that went along with her passion for dancing. And boy, could she dance. There was an extraordinarily high caliber of music and musicianship in Léopoldville, and we hit a number of clubs that first night. I remember the Showboat Nightclub in the Stanley Hotel located at the corner of Avenue Beernaert and Princesse Astrid. It was the hottest spot in town.

A jazz musician by the name of Franco was the popular act then and he and his quintet played throughout Léopoldville in those days. They had helped create a mix of Afro-Cuban music that had apparently been derived from the songs heard on 78s brought in from Cuba. Congolese bands copied the sound and added local tribal beats and an extraordinarily intoxicating rhythm. Gail and Franco and I spent the next several evenings together.

Her moves went right alongside the quality of the music. I did a quick study in order to try and keep up with her, but dancing with her, holding her hand while she whirled before me, was the ultimate antidote to the illness I'd been through. Even if by comparison my footwork didn't measure up, that didn't stop us from closing down the best clubs in the Congolese capital for three consecutive nights.

We'd dine at Léopoldville's finest restaurants and then she would dance and I would stumble along, all night, until the African sunrise accompanied us home in the morning.

After those three days and nights I showed up again at Johnson's office. He looked up from his paperwork and he seemed startled. "You look worse than when you arrived," he said. "What the hell have you been doing?"

I smiled. "Just a little R and R," I replied. He gave me a long, silent stare. "Get your ass on that airplane back to Albertville in the morning and get on with the war," he ordered, then went back to his work.

My meeting with Johnson signaled the end of a pretty good trip to Léopoldville, all things considered. I enjoyed a respite from the challenges of fighting the Simbas and I retreated from death's door. And along the way I was privileged to spend a few days in the company of a dancer, full of life and rejuvenating energy, which was exactly what I needed. There was one thing I didn't have to worry about: the Force Navale Congolaise would be there, waiting for me when I returned.

Several months later I was back in Léopoldville for a briefing. There was a gathering at the embassy where I met a missionary doctor and surgeon. He'd been in Congo for several years by then and was working closely with the Congolese government and even with Mobutu himself. As a matter of fact, he would later become Mobutu's personal physician. We got to talking and I told him about the fever I had experienced. He was a good listener and followed my description closely. Then he nodded solemnly. "Sounds like you survived dengue hemorrhagic fever," he said.

He went on to explain that the infection also bears the quaint alternate name of "breakbone fever," which is a perfect term, because that's exactly the description of how I felt at the height of my illness. Later I would learn more about dengue. It's a tropical disease transmitted by several different species of mosquito within the genus *Aedes*. It's become a global problem since WWII and is endemic in more than 110 countries. It's caused by the dengue virus and in a small proportion of cases it can develop into the life-threatening dengue hemorrhagic fever, or the ominous-sounding dengue shock syndrome.

The missionary doctor I'd met at the embassy became quite an expert on tropical viral diseases. In 1976, he played a vital role in the first outbreak of a newly discovered, extremely deadly virus, one that sprang up in the rural village of Yambuku along the Ebola River. He was instrumental in containing that initial outbreak of Ebola, quarantining several villages and helping to recruit the Congolese Air Force to deliver medical personnel and life-saving supplies to remote locations.

The doctor's name was William Close. He spent sixteen years in Congo before he returned to the States and practiced medicine as a self-described "country doctor." He died at his Wyoming home in 2009. He was also the father of actress Glenn Close.

Chapter Thirteen

Cuban Communists versus Cuban Americans

I've kept the original ship's logbook from the Swifts for the past fifty years and I'm not sure why. It contains all the data from those lake patrols and is an artifact of the Cold War now. It has a stiff, weathered yellow cover and a spine held together by cellophane tape reinforced with glue that is blackening around the edges.

The log lays out in handwritten notes the details of precise times and dates as required for any naval officer in command of a vessel. The elements are clearly noted in accordance with the time-honored tradition of maintaining an accurate log: the times of departure, the amount of fuel then and at the return, the run times on the engines, the last oil change. Bearings, headings, intentions for the patrol. It's all entered with care and structure.

Within those notes Chavez reveals the story of this lake conflict. His daily record listed under "Purpose of Trip" chronicles our time in the Congo perfectly. It could sometimes be a mundane routine of patrols and boat and engine maintenance, but then interspersed within those common acts are recurring, provocative notations of enemy fire and contact. The reports range from villagers in danger and the patrols' attempts to help them to other more disturbing events connected to the war.

As the events of late 1965 unfolded and Che Guevara's Congo mission came crashing down, it's possible to track developments back and forth through both our logbook and Guevara's writings in his book.

The opening line of his book, *The African Dream: The Diaries of a Revolutionary War in the Congo*, is: "This is the history of a failure."[12] And it was our Navy that made it so.

After Albertville had been recaptured and taken back from the rebels in the spring, they had moved north up the lake and made the peninsula of the Fizi region their stronghold. While the early summer attack at Fizi Baraka staged by Hoare and the Agency operative McKay had not been a crushing blow to a loosely organized Simba force on the whole, it had severely weakened the Simba defenses.

Following the raid and our battles with their supply boats, Che and his followers were in disarray, struggling to gain recruits and maintain their position. The increasing momentum of our interdiction operations was relentless. By late autumn that year, our fighting came into its most intense phase as we increased pressure on the rebels' abilities to recruit and fight.

At that time, the Simba Rebel forces were clearly breaking down. Guevara grouses throughout his diaries about inaccurate battle information, inappropriately trained troops, desertions and drunkenness, and nonexistent communication. He writes that the Congolese troops are weak and the Cubans have to do it all themselves.

It was very late in the game by then, and Guevara and the rebels were searching for a new base of operations, constantly making attempts to improve relations with the inhabitants of the Fizi region, trying to strengthen the rebel following. But very few locals actually signed up for their revolution.

Advancing enemy troops, the mercenaries and Congolese, were blanketing the area and our systematic, sustained lake interdictions forced the rebels to remain on the move, their numbers steadily dwindling from casualties and desertion, as well as being victimized by their own infighting.

Guevara's army suffered from a scarcity of competent leadership and lack of organization, according to his writings. His group was continually outmaneuvered by the 5 Commando mercenaries that he refers to as guardsmen. "I was informed that a large number of guardsmen where outflanking us from the hills . . . Only one unit did honour to our army and resisted for another hour." He continues, "From a military point of view, the situation is difficult in that our troops are collections of armed men without the slightest discipline and without any fighting spirit . . ."[13]

And he notes that their chief concern was lack of food, a clear signal that our interdiction raids were coming to bear more immediately on the rebels' capabilities. Guevara describes their attempts to hold an area called Nganja, which gave them access to their base at the far end of the lake, and how that critical area was blocked for them, "now that the lake was more and more cut off and food was running short."[14]

In a telegram back to Cuba he wrote, "Enemy pressure increasing and attempt to block lake continuing. Substantial Congolese funds urgently required to prevent isolation."[15]

In October, Che wrote a long letter back home to Fidel Castro. In it he describes his frustrations with the situation and poor capabilities of the available troops. Much of the funds to support the rebel fighting force had come from the government of Tanzania via the lake port of Kigoma, which bordered Lake Tanganyika across from the Congo.

Castro had also been financing the rebel activity quite aggressively, and Che found fault with that strategy. In his letter, he advises Castro not to send any more money. He reasons that without it the fighters will be dependent on him for their supplies and food and not simply walk away from the fight once they are paid. Guevara chastises Castro as if he were an errant child: "Don't make the mistake again of dishing out money like that; for they cling to me when they feel hard up and certainly won't pay me any attention if the money is flowing freely."[16]

The poor condition of the boats available to the rebels was also a concern for the Cuban revolutionary leader. Guevara complains that of three Soviet ferries that arrived over a month ago, two are already out of commission, and the third is "leaking all over the place." He suggests that an additional three Italian launches will end up in the same state unless Fidel sends Cuban crews to maintain them. The lack of seaworthiness of these craft was directly attributable to the skirmishes and raids our teams made against the rebels on the water.

Despite all the speculation back in Washington, the real situation on the ground in the Congo was quite different from what DC perceived. Early on, no one there realized there were Cubans fighting on the communist side, or that the US was inadvertently contributing to a Cuban-against-Cuban battlefield.

That configuration of combatants came out of the desire for the US government to maintain a covert mission and to counter the Soviet and Chinese assistance to the rebels using Cubans instead of American personnel. It included our Navy, and another formidable force. The CIA had built a massive Air Force, and the air campaign was critical to our mission success. A training program that had begun as early as 1961, at the request of the Congolese, grew into a superb Air Force piloted solely by Cuban exiles.

The first Cuban pilots arrived in the Congo in 1962, and they eventually numbered in the hundreds, initially flying AT-6s borrowed from the Congolese military. Later they switched to US-supplied T-28s and by '64 they had a fully ramped up base of operations, complete with C-47 transports, heavy-duty helicopters, parts and machinists, all in support of this substantial Air Force. The pilots were recruited by the US government under the supervision of the CIA and were paid modest salaries, augmented by combat pay and life insurance policies.

They became known as "Makasi pilots," and according to Frank Villafaña in his book *Cold War In The Congo*, the name means "strong" and "powerful" and was given to them by the Congolese Army.

These hundreds of pilots flew throughout the Congo with missions ranging from support in stabilizing the government (their mere presence in the air was often sufficient) to more targeted actions like bombing and firing raids against rebel advances.

The mighty Makasi Air Force was eventually given a much broader mission. They were authorized to attack truck convoys and dive-bomb arms depots wherever they found sites. The more aggressive air tactics weren't just ad-hoc measures; they were requested by the embassy and approved all the way up the chain, including by McGeorge Bundy, the president's special assistant for National Security, Under Secretary of State George Ball, and Under Secretary of State for Political Affairs Averell Harriman. By early 1965, their air assaults were dominating the region.

As the pilots progressively proved their worth in the Congo campaign, the government saw to it that aircraft manufacturer Douglas upgraded their equipment. According to Villafaña, a B-26K was designed for extra range and more fire power, and was built expressly in response to Makasi pilots' reluctance to fly the first-generation B-26. The new planes were equipped with twice as many machine guns and rockets as the T-28 and quickly became the aircraft of choice in which Makasi pilots ruled the air.

Planes strafed the rebel positions continually as the T-28 and B-26s soared overhead and dove down taking precise aim on rebel convoys and encampments.

Our air and naval dominance was decisive. At the end of October, Guevara writes in his diary that it had been a period of "unmitigated disaster," particularly because of the "shameful fall at Baraka, Fizi . . ." and at two other locations.

His only slightly upbeat notion came from the consequences of an airstrike that killed thirty cows near a small village where the rebels were able to make several good meals from the corpses. Meat was a commodity that was in extremely short supply at that point.

The efforts of the mighty Makasi Air Force overhead, and our radar-enhanced Navy patrols on the lake, were making a material difference. As a combat team, from the air and from the water, we had the rebels in a very tight box, and knew that we and the Makasi pilots were making an impact, both tangible and psychological. Che and his cohorts knew the same thing, and were seeing their mission begin to fall apart.

In a report back to Castro, whom they code-named Rafael, Che details the ways in which the Tanzanian government could further assist them in their fight. Guevara proposes that a high-level delegation of Cubans visit Tanzania and offer unlimited and unconditional financial aid.

His plan was that the Tanzanian government also be asked to maintain tele-communications and to allow regular, twice-weekly shipments of supplies and mail to be delivered by boat.

Perhaps his thinking was that Tanzanian-flagged craft would not be subject to the attacks by our Navy. He proposed that the Tanzanian government bring him two speedboats and deliver a one-time shipment of weapons.

He justifies this request by again referring to the poor quality of the Soviet ferries, particularly against the quality of the Force Navale Congolaise, specifically referring to the fact that we had speedboats. He tells Castro that his men have been wounded and their craft have been damaged in these lake attacks, and that their boats attempt the lake crossings in twos, because inevitably, one of their boats breaks down and must be towed by the other. But he also acknowledges that there are flaws in his plan.

He recognized that Tanzania would certainly not allow its boats to remain on the Congo side of the lake. It's clear that this arrangement would mean those boats would see daily combat because he understood that our patrols would engage them once their real purpose was discovered. Che suggests that the boats remain with his men on "his" side of the lake to utilize the boats to ferry supplies on a nightly basis.

He also requests that one of the boats must be able to be transported over steep mountains, ala *Fitzcarraldo,* the character in the Werner Herzog film, in case "we lose control of the lakeside," Guevara writes.

In his letter, Che asks Fidel to insist that he and his troops be able to retain a clandestine area in Tanzania where these borrowed lake craft can land and pick up supplies during the night, then sail away back toward his stronghold before dawn. But even with any hope of victory crashing down around him, Guevara is careful to cover his tracks. He tells Fidel that it is "advisable to give the Soviets and the Chinese a copy of the final text, to forestall any maneuver to discredit us."[17]

In a late November message from a Rwandan Colonel, Joseph Mundandi, whose men had been fighting alongside the Congolese Rebels and Cubans for several months, Che receives a reality check on the situation regarding local peasant support.

"The local population has already sold out and given cows to the enemy soldiers. The enemy is better guided and has better intelligence about our position than we have ourselves . . . I have decided to call a retreat . . . I am not abandoning the Cuban comrades but I must assume my responsibility toward the Rwandan people."[18]

Then, a devastating message arrived from Dar es Salaam: Tanzania had decided to withdraw their financial support of the Cuban forces.

From both comrade soldiers and sponsoring governments, the ability of the rebels to continue to foster their revolution was dwindling, and not simply by the withdrawal of Mundandi's Rwandan troops and Tanzania's finances. Simba leader Kabila himself wrote to Che about the "crushing of our struggle," and he warned, "there is no money."[19]

The Congolese rebel fighters were also deserting the cause. Oscar Fernandez Mell, one of Che's closest friends and a member of the Central Committee of the Communist Party of Cuba who had fought alongside Che in the Sierra

Maestra mountains during the revolution, received a devastating message from one of Che's deputy leaders: ". . . I think I have lost my nerve. We are forcing men who don't want to fight, and I don't think that makes sense."[20]

Che writes in his book that by mid-November, "the lake was more and more cut off and food was running short." And finally, his diary entry complained that "the supply ship is not crossing the lake because it did not have anything to bring."[21]

Despite these weaknesses and setbacks, Guevara's Cuban forces continued to hold onto their lakeside base until late November when the Congolese Guardsmen, as Che continually refers to them, had broken through at their Upper Base camp and Guevara's men there had retreated.

There had been air strikes in advance of this attack and the guard on duty at the rebel camp had not seen the enemy until it was too late. Guevara heard that they were advancing in three columns. He almost immediately contacted one of his commanders and proposed to organize full retreat. Once the word "retreat" was spoken, "chaos reigned supreme at the base,"[22] he writes.

After Mundandi and the Rwandan troops withdrew, it was only days before the Congolese fighters themselves abandoned their posts altogether.

In the final days of Che Guevara's ill-fated Congo campaign, he was left alone with only his Cuban comrades who had come halfway around the world and ended up fighting against other Cubans.

Ultimately, Che seemed to recognize the futility of his position. "Could I ask the Cubans to die in the trenches to defend this piece of nothing?" he questions. He then sent another message by radio to Fidel Castro. "Rafael: Things are falling apart. Whole units and peasants are going over to the enemy . . . crew and boats in good condition urgently needed."[23]

Che's calamity was nearly finished in the Congo.

Chapter Fourteen

Che Abandons the Fight. We Do Not.

Our success on the lake was in no small measure due to the fact that we had the best Cuban enginemen and boat crews on our side. Guevara's forces were short on everything: talent, skills, conviction, and inspiration. The speed with which his own Cubans were becoming disheartened was alarming to Guevara.

Guevara writes that his fleet captain, Changa, has increasing difficulty crossing the lake because "each time there were more boats keeping watch." Two days later the final evacuation of the Guevara Cuban forces began, on the night of November 18, 1965.

At dawn the next day, Guevara reports that they set fire to the house where they made their camp and were preparing the evacuation. They would move from the area of Kibamba to Jungo, approximately three hours' march. They were edging toward a rendezvous point where boats would pick them up and ferry them across the lake to the safety of Tanzania, effectively ending Guevara's efforts in Congo.

Che sent a message to Changa at the port in Kigoma, Tanzania. He transmitted their position and asked that Changa leave Kigoma as soon as possible.

Che writes that at that time Changa had difficulty on the lake because of enemy aircraft flying over during that entire day. In the afternoon, Che finally made contact again with Changa. Che radioed that fewer than two hundred men would be evacuated, and that they were ten to fifteen kilometers south of Kibamba.

And then Che received Changa's response. "The crossing is set for tonight. Yesterday the commissioner did not let us cross."

The local commissioners often controlled the areas where the rebels made their camps, and perhaps that commissioner had been aware of our boats tenaciously patrolling up and back, curtailing enemy action on the lake, fulfilling the exact tenet of our mission.

In the ship's log of November 19, Chavez made a notation at 17:15 that afternoon. He writes, "We received instructions to patrol from Balukala to Jungo because rebel boats are maneuvering in the area." Lobo-1 and Lobo-2 both went up to Jungo at exactly that time. Normally we left one of the Swifts at base, the crews of the standby boat ready to depart, fuel topped off, weapons clean, rations and water stowed. But on that day, both Swifts were in action because we knew how close we were to catching the enemy leaders, meaning Che himself. Our boats were right on top of the rebels, which necessitated both Swifts being out on the lake that day.

One of the Swifts was about eight nautical miles off shore, the other just four. They then broke off into different directions and continued to patrol the area with search radar.

According to Guevara, he and his fleeing rebels reached Jungo in time for bed and things were chaotic. There was no food, and a head count revealed that four of his men were missing, including a man from the Upper Base who had inexplicably disappeared. They put together what he refers to as a "limited defense" and "continued on our way towards Sele, a village quite close to Jungo."[24]

The next afternoon, Lobo-1 Captain Ricardo Chavez's ship's log reports that "I have been informed . . . from Commandant Peters of the 5th Commando that the rebels are abandoning Jungo area, that they (5 Commando) are going to Baraka to intercept them by land because they are running away toward N.W. He also told me to go to Jungo area because they had received information of rebel boats trying to cross the lake from Jungo to Tanzania."

Chavez and crew had the right information and were in the correct area. In the ship's log, he reports that on the night of November 19 at 22:00 hours, they stopped the engines and continued to listen and keep up their radar search three nautical miles off shore from Jungo.

That same day Guevara cables his lieutenant, Changa: "We have lost the base, we are proceeding with emergency equipment, reply urgently whether you can come tonight."

The next day, November 20, Guevara and Changa finally meet up and the evacuation of the remnants of his troops begins. This is the same day that Chavez and the crew of Lobo-1 witnessed a Makasi plane on a steep dive that came crashing into the lake.

The November 20 entry in the ship's log describes what the crew of Lobo-1 witnessed. The engines were off and the Swift was anchored near an area that Chavez records as Kasimia Bay. Felix Toledo remembers the afternoon well. "There were two planes overhead," he says. "And they approached like they were going to attack." It's possible that they thought our boats were rebel ships, and they were coming down to take a look.

Chavez notes in the log that about 12:15 that afternoon, "we see an airplane coming down." Toledo remembers they thought the planes were going to shoot, but nothing happened. One plane dove and pulled up and veered away. But the other plane, in a steep dive, just kept on coming, never pulled up. It struck the lake with tremendous force, creating a violent splash as the plane hit the water.

Suddenly there were numerous planes in the area and they began to circle over the spot where the Makasi pilot had gone in. Chavez started the engines and they headed toward the crash site. It took only about fifteen minutes for Lobo-1 to cover the distance. Lobo-2 was also out on patrol that day and they arrived at the crash site shortly after Lobo-1. It was not our protocol for both Swifts to be out on the lake at the same time, but this day was different.

Toledo remembers that the crew of Lobo-1 stayed in the area for quite a while, circling around until finally they saw a wheel from the plane bob to the surface, and then a portion of the landing gear. Then a helmet, and some papers. "It was shocking," he said. "Like there was no reason why such a thing should happen."

Ricardo and the crew retrieved the pilot's body from the water. Shortly thereafter, they saw a rescue boat come on the scene. It was Cassidy, and a few of our other men, coming out to help with the rescue.

Following the shock of the plane crash, Toledo remembers that later, back at port in Albertville, some of the Makasi pilots tried to reason it out. Our Cuban crew and the Cuban pilots spent a good deal of time together when they were off duty. They had developed some close relationships and they frequently had dinner together. All of them were there for the same reason, the fight against communism, so they had a natural kinship.

Toledo says the pilots explained that when you are up in the air and flying over water it can reflect and make it seem as though the water is very far away, when it actually is not. They thought this illusion might have been what caused that pilot to crash.

The pilot was a Frenchman named Jacques Roques, according to the reports that survive from that incident. Chavez remembers Roques spoke Spanish very well and consequently spent a lot of time with the Cubans and had developed quite a close friendship with some of them. Seeing the accident was a sad reminder of the capriciousness of warfare and the fleeting nature of a successful mission.

When Cassidy had arrived at the crash site, he was not only there to help with the rescue, but also to make sure that our Navy crews continued the patrol they were charged with that day.

This is reflected in Ricardo's ship's log, where in his next notation after the plane crash he records the elements of being back to business, patrolling over a wide area of the lake throughout the rest of the day and into the night, until dawn.

The crash may possibly have been just that much of a diversion of the Swift crews' attention, just long enough for Changa to make contact with Che, and for the bedraggled rebel Cuban fighters to board their boats and cross into Tanzania. There is no note in Chavez's ship's log of a sighting of rebel boats on that fateful crossing. While tending to the recovery of a downed fighter pilot, Lobo-1 may have unintentionally opened the escape window, allowing Guevara and company to climb out.

On November 21, still out on patrol somewhere near a site Chavez records as Talama Lubanda, exactly three nautical miles from shore, they spot an unidentified plane. "It's flying over Bele," Chavez writes, and the plane is dropping something into the sky. At 16:40, the plane begins to head away from Chavez's location toward the Tanzania Coast, according to Chavez's log. Then the aircraft makes a 180 degree turn and is "coming toward us, flying very low." Chavez and the men on Lobo-1 were anticipating action. He notes, "All crew is in for the fight." As the plane continues diving toward them, Chavez maneuvered the boat into position, but then the plane veered away, back toward Tanzania. "It now makes circles far away from us . . . near Tanzania coast heading south," he notes. They continue to watch until finally the plane is completely out of sight, and they can no longer see it.

This would have been the day that Guevara and his men were evacuated out of Tanzania. Possibly they were on that plane.

Che Guevara and his ill-fated rebel band had been out of food, money, weapons, supplies, and luck. We ran them out of the Congo. They were sent packing by the combined efforts of the Force Navale Congolaise, the mighty Makasi Air Force, and the 5 Commando mercenary army.

But even with that portion of the rebel forces on the run, our operations against the remaining insurgents continued.

* * *

The events in Congo began to move quickly after the Communist Cuban forces pulled out. That same week on November 25, General Mobutu staged a bloodless coup d'état, which ousted President Kasavubu and Prime Minister Kimba.

A circular telegram on November 26 from the Secretary of State Dean Rusk to all African posts reports: "Mobutu announced he will retain presidential prerogatives for five years, during which Colonel Leonard Mulamba (Military Governor Stanleyville area) will serve as Prime Minister and General Bobozo (Commanding Officer Elisabethville garrison) will be Commander in Chief Armed Forces (probably nominally). Mobutu also claimed support from presidents Congolese Parliament chambers and confirmed them in their positions for five years."[25]

This coup, even though it was accomplished without armed intervention, raised concerns in the US because it meant that the Congolese presidential elections, which had been scheduled for the following March, would be scrubbed.

The coup also created internal Congolese constitutional problems, and even though the US saw it as a way of preventing "political and military disintegration," Mobutu was only thirty-five years old and the constitution required a minimum presidential age of forty. The constitution would have to be amended to accommodate him.

Rusk paints a particularly rosy picture of Mobutu's intentions, noting that he had gained "effective control of machinery of government"[26] and was also not in immediate danger from any overt opposition. The US believed Mobutu had the support of the leaders of both houses of parliament and that he would restore freedom of the press. They also found it a positive sign that Mobutu had not so far enacted any retribution against any of the former leaders. Mobutu had announced that his new government would leave in place and respect all African and international agreements that the country had previously signed onto. Rusk stated in his memo that the "Department will maintain discreet and informal contacts with new leaders pending completion our study this question."[27]

I have said that all of us in the Congo believed that Mobutu was the best option at the time. He was comparatively non-corrupt, had demonstrated leadership skills, acknowledged the failures of his own troops as part of an effort to upgrade its quality and performance, and showed no signs of seeking revenge or retribution for anything in the past.

The corruption and megalomania that would become the standard in his government was not evident at this time in his personal history.

A later telegram from Rusk to the embassy in Belgium on December 1 states, "Assumption of power by Mobutu may be last real opportunity in short-run for Congo to gain political stability which has eluded it since 1960."[28]

There was a general feeling that since the Mobutu coup hadn't generated wholesale outrage and opposition, it demonstrated that everyone, including the Congolese politicians, was tired of the instability.

Other elements were also changing the complexion of our Congo tenure. LCol Mike Hoare had decided not to extend his contract; he would leave the country by the end of November.

But just before he left the Congo he paid a visit to the new president in order to say his goodbyes. Mobutu handed Hoare a letter of thanks in which he expressed his "profound regret" that Hoare will be leaving the Congo, a "nation that owes you a great deal." Hoare left that meeting wishing the new president well and in his book he writes about his feelings toward Mobutu. "If the Congo is to succeed in taking its place amongst the great nations of Africa, it will be largely as a result of the efforts of this great man."[29]

Sadly, Mobutu's own subsequent corruption would render Hoare's sentiments empty. But Hoare's comments do reflect the almost unanimous acclamation of Mobutu's behavior at the time.

Later, in mid-December 1965, the Chief of Station, Larry Devlin, sent a note back to CIA Headquarters expressing his opinion that Mobutu was a moderate and pro-West option who would be willing to "accept advice." Even though he maintained that the coup was the "only feasible solution to the political crisis," there were other concerns on Devlin's mind. He didn't want all of the responsibility for the successful outcome of a Mobutu takeover to fall on the CIA alone. He called for other US government agencies to take action. He warned that if they failed to do so, or that if the Congolese themselves didn't take "the necessary steps," everyone could face a new crisis that could potentially be even more destructive to the Congo and to US interests in Africa.

This meant that the CIA and Devlin remained committed to our missions. The Agency would continue "devoting considerable time and energy to operations designed to provide early warning, should the opposition try to launch another coup d'état."[30] Devlin recognized that what we were doing provided the US government with not only a combat force against the rebels, but also an intelligence-gathering service. Devlin emphasized that our operations would continue "in an effort to shore up and assist the present government."[31]

Because of this belief, our operation continued into January and February of 1966.

A late December status update on the Congo situation was sent from the Deputy Director of African Affairs to the Assistant Secretary of State for African Affairs. It was the call to continue the action of our Navy and the air campaign owing to the fact that rebel activity was still being detected in the region around Albertville and farther north.

The deputy director reported that our military campaign against the rebel concentration in the Fizi area had been expected to end the last major threat by the rebels. But he noted that the campaign was still ongoing and that we had achieved successes in recapturing territory. He then wrote: "Nevertheless, recent reports from the Congo indicate significant rebel activity in the region around Albertville, the Northeast sector, and the Stanleyville area."

The US government had not yet realized that Che and his Cubans had left the country, as evidenced by this dispatch reference in the same memo: "Foreign advisory assistance is probably a factor, but none of the Cubans alleged to accompany rebel forces in the East has been captured. Support from neighboring countries has diminished considerably over the past several months." This we know from Che's conversations with Castro about the Tanzanian government withdrawing its financial support.

In a February 5, 1966 memorandum from the 303 Committee, the high-level group within the US government that approved and supervised our covert activities, there was a request to continue the funding of our work. The maritime operation is the first item on the agenda.

"1) [*less than one line not declassified*] maritime activities in the Congo be maintained at their present level through June 30, 1966, after which [*less than one line not declassified*] participation would be sharply reduced. The reduction may be possible earlier (and would then be greater) if even before that date the Congolese Government accepts responsibility for crewing the boats."[32]

The 303 Committee memo makes direct reference to our boats having had action against the rebels the previous November. The memo confirms that there are still large rebel bands north of Albertville, which continued to mount successful ambushes against Central Government forces. It mentions that Sudan, Tanzania, and Uganda have officially ceased their support of the rebel activities, but that as late as November 1965, "a small action was fought at night between boats belonging to the [*less than one line not declassified*] maritime unit on Lake Tanganyika and rebel boats approaching the Congo from the Tanzanian shore."[33]

Chavez's account gives more detail on the action. On the night of November 23, Chavez records in his ship's log a combat encounter with five rebel boats. His entry states that at 20:15 they discovered five boats heading toward Tanzania.

He writes, "I entered into the middle of the bunch of boats making a high firing." The boats began to exchange fire, Chavez noting that they were taking shots from "all posts around us." He was concentrating on the radar while maneuvering Lobo-1 and supervising the boat crew, a man on each weapon—the .50 cal machine guns mounted mid-ship, port, starboard, and aft, and shoulder-fired submachine guns wherever needed to augment the .50s.

Chavez's ship's log notes give us a representation of what the night battle was like, with Chavez noting that two boats turned at some point during the battle and began to head west toward shore, and that the other three spread out but were headed toward the Tanzanian coast. "We chased the two boats heading west," he writes. "And interrupt their escape toward the west shore. Now, they begin to run." Chavez and crew continued to chase these boats, firing continually.

Assuming the Swifts were firing two machine guns at a rate of fire of 750 rounds per minute per gun, that would have been 1,500 rounds per minute from both, which were firing intermittently, depending upon the position of the Swift and the positions of the bandits. Then add the rounds from the AK-47s at 600 rounds per minute on full automatic, and the amount of ammunition consumed was impressive. No wonder the rebel boats didn't stand much of a chance.

Then there was a change in tactic. One of the three boats that was headed toward the Tanzanian coast stopped and turned around; it stayed in an area for a while and then began firing at Lobo-1 and crew. The bow submachine gun operator of Lobo-1 took a bullet in his right foot and Chavez reports that the 57mm had hit its target three times, a bright white flash being the clear sign that their fire was accurate. The battle continued with the Swift crew firing on the two other boats that were by this time only a short distance away. And then the returning fire stopped.

The capricious nature of this kind of combat can always be identified by the things that go wrong, particularly at a crucial moment. Right then, Chavez and crew had an equipment failure. The radio operator turned on his set so that he could to report back to the base. Chavez's log book states: "a white light, almost like a short circuit" erupted from the equipment. All their 12-volt lights were blown out and the radio went dead. They couldn't raise anyone on VHF.

Radio operator Felix Toledo continued trying to make contact with base while the rest of the crew remained focused on the two remaining boats, keeping up their fire, even though the enemy boats were still not returning fire. Finally, with a wounded man onboard, Chavez made the decision to withdraw and go to back to base so they could seek medical treatment for his injured crewman.

The memo from the 303 Committee reports that the US government was concerned about supporting Mobutu and making sure he stayed in power, thus the request of the continued funds was approved. The memo made specific reference to the effects our Force Navale Congolaise were having on the situation, and to this encounter Chavez and crew had that night:

"The boats have been used extensively in interdiction patrols to prevent supplies and men from reaching rebels fighting on the eastern shore of Lake Tanganyika and to prevent rebels from escaping across the lake to Tanzania . . . it is known that two Soviet-supplied 35-foot armed launches have been on the lake since September 1965. As a result of the Congolese maritime force (our Navy), most of the traffic between Tanzania and the rebels has had to move by night. In November 1965, the Congolese force engaged five rebel craft after dark, apparently proceeding from Tanzania to the Congo. Throughout the current military campaign against the last centers of organized rebel resistance in the eastern Congo, the boats have carried out reconnaissance patrols, escorted other boats transporting personnel, supplies of food, ammunition and arms; and evacuated wounded. The presence of the boats on the lake has continued to have a salutary effect on the morale of the local population, both African and European."

As the Cubans continued to crew the Swifts assisted by the 5 Commando mercenaries, the US government was still concerned about a Cuban presence in the Congo. The February 5 memo records, "continuing efforts to find suitable replacements for the [*less than one line not declassified*] crews of the Swifts . . . it is expected that several European seamen will be recruited shortly and proceed to Albertville."

Through this period, according to declassified documents, the Department of State continued trying to find replacements for the Cubans and pursued the possibility of gradually turning over responsibility of the boats to Congolese troops and mercenaries and utilizing them exclusively as the crew. It was expected that this process would not take very long and that in the "near future (Congolese and mercenaries) would assume most of the duties now carried out by [*less than one line not declassified*] (Cubans)."

US government officials saw an added benefit that would lower the costs of the operation. If 5 Commando mercenaries or Congolese were to take responsibility, it would reduce the amount needed to fund the maritime program. The planning by the 303 Committee concerning the replacement of the Cubans with mercenaries was well advanced in Albertville and was going as smoothly as possible under the circumstances.

While the Cubans made up the training cadre for our Navy, they were still in the fight, almost daily, and risking their lives to make a success of it. In the December 21 log entry, it's reported that Lobo-1 left our base port at 4:00 that morning heading for the Baraka Peninsula. At 5:00 that afternoon they shut down the engines and waited for dark. Their target was a place called Mboko.

At 7:00 p.m. they began approaching shore until they were one and a quarter nautical miles from Mboko. Reaching their target, Lobo-1 opened fire. Immediately Lobo-1 received return fire from what seemed to be a .30 caliber, Chavez reports, and he ordered his men to stop firing for a few minutes while everyone listened. Then he writes, "I can easily hear the firing of many rifles . . ." and again he ordered his men to continue fire.

The rebels kept up their assault, but we learn from the log that they were not using tracers. The exchange of gunfire went on for another half hour before Chavez ordered a ceasefire. They pulled away, heading southeast. At 10:30 that night they reported a string of very bright lights on shore. They slowed the engines and went in closer to investigate. Chavez believed they were lights from Greek fishing boats that worked up and down Lake Tanganyika, such as those my friend Tasos managed, since the lights seemed to be coming from something located very close to shore, and the radar wasn't giving an echo.

At this point Lobo-1 was only one nautical mile off shore. Chavez and the crew then withdrew and took their Swift Boat about four miles out, and there they waited until dawn.

Through the course of the night it began to rain, hard. There was absolutely no visibility and there were no longer any lights discernible. At 4:00 a.m. they began to patrol again, searching for the lights that had been there earlier. They patrolled the area for another two hours but as the sun came up they lost any chance of spotting those lights again. Chavez wrote of how bright the lights had been, and speculated that they might have even been Coleman lanterns. With a tenacity that I remember well, he details his plan to return there later in the evening looking for any indication of lights from potential enemy boats on the lake.

They waited, still hoping to see those lights, but when no illuminations were spotted on the shore, the crew headed south, back to their previous target at the other end of the peninsula. There they found clusters of lights in two groups. When the crew was ordered to make a high fire, all the lights in both groups suddenly went out. Chavez ordered the crew to fire again, and there they found the enemy.

A rapid exchange of gunfire erupted between the boats and the enemy on shore. For nearly an hour Chavez and his crew were embroiled in a ship-to-shore battle, using all weapons on board, until Chavez's log finally records, "They don't shoot anymore." Lobo-1 had taken out an enemy stronghold. They had been out on the lake for a little more than twenty-four hours and had engaged in two serious gunfights, attacked on the water and from the shore.

Lobo-1 and crew then headed south just after midnight. At 3:00 a.m. they switched out the fuel tanks and began to run on the forward tank. At 7:00 a.m. they finally reached a place we referred to as the Islands, a sheltering area near our base where the crews would stop over to clean the boats and their weapons.

The Cuban crew of Lobo-1, after doing battle against the communist rebels, performed these routine tasks and finally headed for home. It had been three days since they left our base. They pulled into port in Albertville at 10:00 on the morning of December 24, just in time for the most bizarre Christmas I believe any of us has ever spent.

* * *

When I began the project of writing this book, I opened the ship's logbook for the first time in years. I found a note, one page of lined paper torn from a looseleaf binder, lying inside the front cover. The note is addressed to me. I don't remember reading it at the time, but seeing it nearly a half a century later, written with a little bit of phonetic "Spanglish," I found it a gracious parting gift from the crew. "Chief," it says, "We give you good year. 1966. Employees of Force Navy. Kivu. Kapitan R. Chavez. Albertville, ce 1.9.66" Ricardo and his men had indeed handed me, and all of us concerned, a very good year.

Chapter Fifteen

Corruption in the Congo

These days would also mark the end of Mike Hoare's tenure as head of the mercenary army fighting in the Congo. Hoare's contract had expired and he felt as though the war was essentially won, and there were just mopping-up skirmishes to follow. Our crews discovered that this was not the case at all, and we spent the next several months chasing down a ragtag, but determined, rebel force still capable of putting up a fight.

Hoare had elected not to extend his time. He was exhausted from the energy-sapping heat and humidity of the equatorial tropics, and was most likely feeling the pressures. In his book *Congo Mercenary,* he writes, "I wanted only the adventure and the fulfillment of command."[34]

He was tired of making decisions surrounded by uncertainty, of juggling various political interests, and he was also frustrated with the deteriorating quality of the 5 Commando personnel, which had never been very high to begin with. Over the course of his time in the Congo, the military unit had declined further.

He also had his young wife and infant son in tow for much of his campaigning, and they were ready to depart from the discomfort of constant threat and frequent camp moves.

One of Hoare's most effective commanders was John Peters. He was a trusted collaborator, and as Cassidy confided to me, he and Peters had been responsible for securing Hoare's portion of any resources the 5 Commando liberated during their raids. Peters was an ex-NCO who was said to have a "fanatical prejudice" against the British officer class. He was also a ruthless killer and may have been a deserter from the British Army.

Peters's accomplishments as the premier 5 Commando combat officer made him LCol Hoare's obvious designated replacement. However, as the war wound down, the changed circumstances may have dictated a different type of officer was more suitable to head 5 Commando. Major Hugh van Oppen, a man of considerable military bearing, was Peters's potential rival for the command. Peters and van Oppen were like oil and water.

Van Oppen was textbook perfect as a British officer. Tall and handsome with an upper-crust British accent, and he had attended the Royal Military Academy at Sandhurst. But a court-martial there deprived him of an illustrious British military career.

The incident at Sandhurst involved a roommate's stolen camera. Van Oppen was acquitted in the court martial but was "disciplined" by being returned to his unit to fight in Korea and Egypt rather than being allowed to graduate from Sandhurst. He went on to serve in the Royal Regiment in Korea, and later as a press officer in Egypt before leaving the military in 1956. His next stop was the Northern Rhodesia Police, where he commanded a riot squad platoon.

After that he served in the Federal Army with the Royal Rhodesia Regiment during the 1959 State of Emergency in Nyasaland and played the key role in quelling the most serious riot there at Nkata Bay.

Van Oppen also worked in intelligence gathering for the Rhodesian federal government along the Northern Rhodesia-Katanga border and elsewhere in the Congo, which is where he came in contact with Hoare.

After briefly returning to England, he went to Holland where he worked as a stevedore in the Rotterdam docks. Eventually he joined Hoare's 5 Commando and performed admirably. But as a warrior, compared to the ruthless Peters, who may have been short on style but had proven bravery and battlefield competence, van Oppen was a bit of a tea-sipper. His upper-crust British officer image rankled Peters, who despised van Oppen. And the feeling was mutual.

Even the possibility of van Oppen taking over as Hoare's successor would have been intolerable to Peters. He always saw himself as the entitled heir-apparent and Peters would have considered the most ruthless set of tactics perfectly justifiable, much like Jock Cassidy. Everyone in the Congo who had anything to do with 5 Commando had no doubt that Peters was the suspicious hand in an extremely messy final act for van Oppen.

There is a lot of confusion and speculation, but very little consensus and no substantive investigation, about what happened to Hugh van Oppen on the night of May 8, 1966. Dawn would find van Oppen dead with a number of bullets in his stomach.

In Anthony Mockler's book *The New Mercenaries*, he writes, "Peters's version of events apparently was that van Oppen attempted to murder him, and on failing, committed suicide."[35] Peters never had a sense of humor, but this version is hilarious in its absurdity, and is also in keeping with the story I know and that circulated while I was still in Albertville. It was openly whispered, with a generous helping of derision, that van Oppen accidentally killed himself. But the circumstances would make that inevitability extremely unlikely, if not impossible.

It was reported that van Oppen shot himself with a full burst from his own weapon while cleaning the gun. But an "accident" of that sort would have been very difficult to accomplish, because a full burst would require the improbable assumption that his finger got stuck on the trigger and held it down as the clip emptied into his belly.

According to Colin Baker, Professor Emeritus at the University of Glamorgan (now University of South Wales), in his biography, *Wild Goose: The Life and Death of Hugh van Oppen,* he had visited his brother Martin in South Africa just a month prior to that fatal night, and Martin reported that Hugh van Oppen was "profoundly worried about something."[36] He dreaded returning to the Congo, according to his brother, because something there was making van Oppen uncomfortable, something that he did not share with his brother. Baker writes that he "feared there was trouble ahead. He really needed someone to cover his back for him."[37]

Speculation is that he, Hoare, and Peters, as well as another 5 Commando leader, had been approached by a group of Belgian landowners about mounting a coup against Mobutu, whom they saw as a CIA puppet. That story line has Peters declining to participate and letting Mobutu know about the plot, and also advising Mobutu that van Oppen was accepting the proposal. From that scenario, Mobutu ordered Peters to kill van Oppen.

I doubt this version of the story. From my experience, it just does not ring true. Mobutu would have told Devlin of any momentous plot like that. I'm including it here but not representing it as anything other than speculation.

In the end, van Oppen really was no match for Peters. Van Oppen looked the role of a British military officer, but he was a powder-puff compared to John Peters, a bit like Little Lord Fauntleroy versus Jack the Ripper.

My opinion? I believe that the odds are 99.99% that Peters had van Oppen killed. Peters was probably calculating enough to have one of his loyal subordinates actually pull the trigger, and I believe that any one of several would have had no qualms about doing the deed.

But even though the circumstances of van Oppen's death are murky with many questions unanswered, Peters was surely threatened by van Oppen. And what is absolutely true is that no one, and that includes me, was shocked when he died and Peters retained his position as head of 5 Commando. There was no one to challenge him. Hoare had already departed and Cassidy had fled after his own bloody disaster forced him from the Congo. Everyone just shrugged and congratulated Peters. His control of 5 Commando was complete and smooth. He was now surrounded by loyal Afrikaners who would never challenge his command. He would remain in charge for nearly another year.

* * *

There were many enterprises going on in the Congo at that time. But they were mostly in contrast to the Greek's creative, well-run ventures such as a hotel and fishing businesses. These other endeavors were of a much more nefarious nature.

The 5 Commando mercenaries, of course, were well positioned to loot the banks and other businesses in the many towns, large and small, that they overran while on the heels of the rebels. And the Congo was endowed with such a wealth of natural resources that it was almost open game for international smugglers and merchants.

Roberto Pichardo, who ran our communications, was at the train station in Albertville one afternoon when he saw, glimmering in the sunlight, a huge bounty of gold bars stacked inside two boxcars. Each was stamped with the name of the mine, and it looked to him like they were being shipped out of the country. Pichardo remembers just how tempting that much gold was, just sitting there, no one else around, no one guarding it at that moment. But he also understood he couldn't take any of it. "What's a guy gonna do with it?" he asked. I would later learn that Cassidy had a use for it.

Ivory was another commodity that drew significant attention in the Congo. One night, an old lake vessel pulled up alongside the quay at the Force Navale Congolaise in Albertville. I remember the ship stood out because it was heavily manned by Congolese military personnel who were wearing uniforms we hadn't seen before.

Naturally, as the local commanding naval force there, we were curious and so we boarded the vessel. We found that the entire cargo hold was filled with ivory tusks. One of the crew told us that it totaled nine tons. If that number was accurate, it's difficult to imagine how many slaughtered elephants that represented.

I pressed the ship's crew repeatedly, trying to find out who owned this irreplaceable treasure. Finally, I was informed that ultimately it belonged to Victor Nendaka, the Chief of Intelligence for the Congolese Government.

Just after Mobutu's successful coup and takeover of the government, he made Nendaka Minister of Transport and Communications. Perhaps this position facilitated his ability to move these goods out of the Congo.

Nendaka was reputedly competent, honest (by the Congolese definition), and very effective. He maintained a low profile and never attempted to take power himself, despite the human, financial, and physical assets that he had under his control.

Apparently, he was also interested in getting rich, regardless of the depredations to the country he was sworn and paid to protect.

Nendaka's behavior and attitude was not unusual in poverty-stricken, developing countries. I recall later, in Indonesia, meeting a very impressive Indonesian fellow married to a Dutch woman. After getting acquainted I asked him why he was honest, while it seemed all of his countrymen were not. He replied that because he was married to a woman with means, he could afford to be. That simple statement puts into perspective a lot of behavior that I had witnessed in Vietnam, Congo, and later in Indonesia. How do you blame a man for not following along with the conventions of corruption if that is what it takes to feed his family, particularly when he sees his leaders doing the same thing on a much larger scale?

Government corruption, of course, allowed many of the riches of the Congo to be exported. It was a country with deep reserves of copper, cobalt, uranium, and diamonds.

I regularly saw smugglers and traders meeting furtively in the dining room of the Hotel Du Lac, ostensibly to facilitate the transfer of diamonds. I say "ostensibly" because we took great care to avoid these people. But we knew they were there and what they were doing. It was the same type of commerce that had existed for decades in the Congo—murky enterprises that took advantage of the country's enormous natural wealth, always executed at the expense of the Congolese people.

In 1971 Mobutu renamed the country Zaire, but the new policies that came with the new name didn't improve living conditions or the economy. For many years the Congo produced more cobalt than any other country in the world. Over the course of Mobutu's corrupt regime, the balance began to change and eventually diamonds surpassed everything as the Congo's main export, including cobalt and copper. Diamonds made up 30 percent of the country's total exports in 1989. But through corruption and financial mismanagement, the entire mining industry was in jeopardy and its share of the GDP went from 11.3 percent in 1988 to 4.7 percent in 1994.

Mobutu's ill-conceived fiscal programs drove the country from bad to worse as the years wore on, even as his personal fortune soared. Over his thirty-two-year reign he was estimated to be worth as much as $5 billion, while almost all facets of life in the Congo deteriorated.

He maintained a "Presidential Services" fund that took up between 17 and 20 percent of the government's budget. He owned personal stock in every enterprise relating to Zaire/Congo, and it was said that no business transaction with a foreign-owned company was allowed to take place unless a kickback was paid to Mobutu personally. He was the largest shareholder in the Banque du Kinshasa and had personal ownership, either partial or outright, in agricultural businesses, mining, and manufacturing in all provinces of the country.

But as Mobutu and his family members and handpicked cronies grew wealthier, the country fell to near ruin. The highway, road, and rail systems were in utter disrepair, the health care system wasn't funded, and human rights violations were rampant.

The World Bank reported that Zaire's per capita income declined at an annual rate of 2.2 percent from 1965 to 1990. And a 2009 Harvard study reported that by "2008 the Democratic Republic of Congo was ranked as the poorest country in the world."[38]

Just a few years before Mobutu would finally leave the scene, according to the same Harvard study, "the country faced a risk of virtual disintegration due to hyperinflation . . . the GDP plummeted, pushing the economy into subsistence agriculture. By the end of 1995, income per capita was only one third its pre-independence levels."[39]

But as 1965 progressed into 1966, we were still prosecuting a war against a group of ruthless Simba Rebels whose philosophy had already demonstrated a capacity for brutality and barbarism that terrified the country, and the world. And when Joseph-Désiré Mobutu showed us many positive traits, like cooperation and leadership, that were not exhibited by any alternative leader who could claim recognition in the hinterlands, the US backed his presidency. By the qualities Mobutu exhibited to us in the moment, no one could have foreseen that his regime would tragically evolve into a megalomaniacal dictatorship, a kleptocracy of global proportions. As incongruous as it seems, Mobutu was clearly the best that was available at that time.

Chapter Sixteen

Tragedy

The end of 1965 brought us the weirdest Christmas any of us had ever experienced. Most of the celebrations took place at the mercenaries' favorite watering hole and barracks, the Palace Hotel, built in the Belgian colonial period, the old hotel was now home to the WIGMO contractors and the Makasi pilots. In the traditional European style, there was a large, club-like room with an "L" shaped, dark ebony wood bar that was about seventy-five feet long and took up most of one side of the room.

This Palace Hotel bar was also the scene of Dern's confrontation with Cassidy, and where later Cassidy murdered an unarmed WIGMO contractor in full view of a dozen witnesses. The place could hardly be called a traditional Christmas setting.

Some of the mercenaries had been out hunting that morning, and one of them had shot a large antelope. The Cuban pilots and Congolese soldiers constructed a large outdoor barbeque in a yard behind the hotel and were roasting the critter on a gigantic makeshift spit for everyone to enjoy. Not exactly figgy pudding and stuffed goose.

Christmas Day and alas, as was often the case, the mercenaries could not control themselves. After far too many drinks, the spirit of the day was lost and things inevitably got far out of hand.

As I've said, I wasn't particularly fond of being around these characters anyway, and especially in their drunken state, so Chavez, Pichardo, and I decided to withdraw early. We were hoping to avoid the usual foul behavior we'd seen too many times as a result of the mercenaries' over-drinking. And we definitely didn't want any of that on Christmas.

As we were departing the watering hole, and before Chavez and Pichardo headed for their house and I went back toward town to the Du Lac, we decided to amble by the Navy barracks ship, just to make sure that the boats had been properly secured prior to the celebrations.

As we made our way across the elevated part of the walkway that ran from the street to the quay where the boats were tied up, we heard noises coming from below. We knew from the commotion that a few of the 5 Commando sailors were down there having a smaller celebration of their own. Suddenly, the sounds of celebration were punctuated by random gunfire, which came uncomfortably close to where we were walking.

It was one of those exceptionally dark nights with no full moon and no illumination along the elevated walkway, so one of us was carrying a flashlight in order to help track our way down the quay and back to port.

When the shots rang out all three of us instinctively hit the deck. Then we heard a few shouts, followed by laughter. A drunken hoot and then more shots. We kept our heads down and waited.

It didn't take long for us to realize that the 5 Commandos were putting on their own special type of Christmas festivities, in their own reckless way. In a drunken haze, they were taking target practice at absolutely nothing, shooting off rounds into the dark just because they could. That dangerous combination of alcohol and guns was again on display in Albertville. As Pichardo referred to it, not friendly fire, just drunken fire.

We immediately began shouting at them, using the profanity that they were most accustomed to. But they couldn't hear us over their hell raising and the gunfire. That was the only thing they were concentrating on. Meanwhile the shots kept coming. Pichardo remembers thinking that they were going to kill us out of sheer stupidity and negligence—a distinct possibility as the shots rang close and hot, with nothing between our heads and a bullet but the two-by-fours of the wooden boardwalk.

Wouldn't it just be a pity to come all this way, to have succeeded this far in a Congo war and to see it nearly won, only to be cut down by a drunken mercenary soldier celebrating Christmas with random gunfire? It was too ridiculous to fathom.

Eventually, in between gunfire and laughter, they heard us and shouted back a few insincere yet perfectly slurred apologies. It was a close call and it seemed as though getting through Christmas safely might be even riskier than some of the actual firefights we'd encountered.

But senseless death had been on our minds anyway, because we had to endure the reality of our own pointless tragedy that had occurred at the end of November. Like every incident resulting in the death of a teammate, it made us all a lot more aware of our own mortality.

It was a cruel element of fate that came into our world on the afternoon of November 28. It would take a major toll on our crew.

At about six o'clock in the evening, a young Congolese corporal named André Menyo was driving a poorly maintained Congolese National Army truck, license plate number 12184. Similar to the old USA M939, the mammoth, 6X6 five-ton, run-down military transport rattled its way along Avenue Storm, the main road running through town toward the Commissary Police Headquarters.

With no warning, the truck sputtered and stopped, stalling directly in front of the Bar Kalemie, just near the Bata Boot Store and a few hundred meters north of the Hotel Du Lac. The truck had been headed in the direction of the port where the Navy base was located, which is probably where the Armee Nationalé Congolaise (ANC) troops were bound for in the first place.

Despite the proximity to my hotel, I'd never been inside the Bar Kalemie. It was one of those dirty, ratty places and a fountain for trouble from which I had always kept my distance.

When Menyo couldn't get the truck started, First Sergeant Kibwabwa ordered everyone out of the back and instructed four of the men to push the truck in an attempt to jump start it. No luck. The truck was too heavy for them to even budge.

Their Ops Bureau, which housed a repair shop, was just a short distance up the road, but since they couldn't move the heavy vehicle, First Sergeant Corporeal Menyo and the rest of the troops abandoned the transport where it had stopped, leaving it jutting precariously out into the street. That section of the roadway was lit by one singularly dim streetlight.

It was Sunday evening. A new moon had occurred just five nights before, so at 1:35 a.m. on Monday it was a pitch-black African night, on a deserted street, with a five-ton hazard lying in wait.

There were no caution lights on the truck, no reflectors, nothing that would mark the presence of an enormous vehicle arbitrarily abandoned on a dark, dry road in the middle of the night.

A pair of 5 Commando mercenary soldiers from South Africa, Hans Von Lieres Und Wilkau and Cornelius Johannes Van Wyk, had been out together that night.

Gooch was with them.

The three of them had driven that road many times and knew the terrain well. Von Lieres was behind the wheel and Gooch was in the shotgun seat. Van Wyk was riding in the back. In the blackness of an African night, with the driver feeling sure of himself, the jeep came racing down that road at a high rate of speed. The official accident report states that the jeep slammed full force into the back of the transport truck, thrusting the truck forward and embedding its front bumper solidly into a coconut palm. The impact also shoved the truck's right front wheel up onto the curb.

The Willys jeep hit the left rear tire of the truck and jammed under the back with such force that it then ricocheted backward slightly, tearing away the truck's axle. It landed with a thud as the tire was sheared away and the body of the truck slammed down, coming to rest on the bare wheel.

Van Lieres lay half inside and half outside the jeep. He was still alive when the first witness ran to the scene. Ferdinand Albert Taminiau lived in the building next to where the accident occurred and the explosive sound of the impact jolted him awake. He'd rushed outside and found Van Lieres "in the throes of death," according to his sworn testimony.

The other South African, Van Wyk, was also still alive and was quickly taken to Roi Albert Hospital for treatment. He remained in the hospital there for four days before he returned home to South Africa. He never came back to the Congo.

Gooch was killed instantly.

I was not informed about the accident until the next morning. When I got the news, I went immediately to where his body had been placed. Cassidy came with me. From some source that is now lost to memory, we found wood and materials and hammered together a coffin. With the assistance of Chavez, Pichardo, and Papo, we wrapped it in strong, heavy canvas and transported it down to the port, where we somehow managed to get a refrigeration unit in one of the warehouses working.

We made sure that Gooch's body was held appropriately until a plane could get to Albertville and make the transport to Léopoldville. There it could be properly prepared for the onward trip back to the USA. Roberto Pichardo remembers that a large group of people arrived in Albertville to accompany the body. "People in uniform, and high-ranking civilians," he says.

Gooch was certainly not the first casualty I had dealt with, but he was the one that affected me the most. Having to handle his body with respect in those extremely crude circumstances was most disheartening. It was my challenge and my responsibility, and we did our best in that terrible situation to get our friend and comrade's body back safely to his family.

His contribution to our mission had been essential. I have carried guilt around for fifty years for obeying my instructions from the Agency not to speak with his wife at the time. In retrospect, it was an exaggerated "security" concern by the Agency. I'm hoping that this book will adequately say what I would have said all those years ago.

In the aftermath of his death, I honored my instructions not to make contact. I understood that there is no predicting how a loved one will react to such tragic news and an inadequate explanation that may by necessity be deliberately vague might exacerbate the grief and threaten operational security. I never felt comfortable remaining silent and until the events were declassified and this book commenced, I had no contact with the Gough family. Now that we are communicating, I can see from my contacts with Gooch's children what a wonderful wife and mother Ida Gough has been, raising them without their father, how proud the children are of their dad, and what a wonderful influence Gooch must have been, just as we knew him in Congo.

The circumstances of Gooch's death are described in the accident report and his death certificate, and I won't recite them here. Taminiau's testimony states that as soon as the casualties were removed from the wreck, he and a few others pushed the jeep to the side of the highway. During the night it caught fire, and like an allegorical funeral pyre, it extinguished the remnants of a life that had contributed value and substance to those of us who would sorely miss his steady presence.

The other mercenary who died in the crash, Von Lieres, of 5 Commando, was one of Mike Hoare's most trusted lieutenants who was wounded twice during previous battles while under Hoare's command. One of those battles was when the Belgians parachuted in from the US C-130s and rescued the Stanleyville hostages in November 1964. In Hoare's book *Congo Mercenary*, he refers to that event as "the most terrifying and harrowing experience of my life."[40]

In that firefight against the rebels, Von Lieres was hit in the leg and took another shot to the head, just behind his ear. The bullet was lodged in his skull, and von Lieres was flown to Johannesburg, South Africa, where doctors removed the bullet. He spent the next few months recovering there and then returned to the Congo to join Hoare's forces once again.

In the spring of 1965, he led an advance against another rebel stronghold and was wounded in the forearm. A few months later Hoare put him on desk duty and claims to have given orders that von Lieres should not be allowed within 100 miles of the front, because he was "definitely accident-prone." It would turn out to be a very prescient comment.

Von Lieres was also with McKay at Fizi Baraka in charge of the PTs that landed troops. I believe that Hoare allowed him back into combat simply because of his courage and his experience. Von Lieres, according to Hoare, dug into a trench and set up a 60mm mortar, opening a searing barrage against the enemy forces, helping to secure a beachhead and give Hoare's troops the upper hand.

Hoare had been in Léopoldville attending ceremonial proceedings with President Kasavubu and taking care of other last-minute details when the jeep accident happened. While he was in Léopoldville, Mobutu had executed his coup, and when Mike Hoare arrived back in our home base of Albertville, he learned that Hans von Lieres and Gooch were dead.

Hoare writes that von Lieres had had a "presentiment of his death only a few days previously."[41] Von Lieres had sent Hoare his resignation and had requested an immediate repatriation back to South Africa. Hoare writes that he willingly approved the request, and felt as though no one could have done more for 5 Commando and for the Congo than von Lieres. He was scheduled to leave the Congo for Johannesburg the next day. One day too late.

Perhaps this is why he and Gooch were out that night. Maybe they were celebrating together, and saying goodbye. It was the end of a successful campaign and a soldier's last night in country before he was scheduled to return home.

The initial report on the accident was filed by Georges Puta, Deputy Police Commissioner of the Albertville Judiciary Police. In a subsequent report, Puta notes that he went to the South African General Staff office in order to obtain the names of the victims of the accident but was told in so many words to "back off." They instructed him that it was a military affair and that he and his office should have nothing to do with it.

The next notation comes the following February, more than two months after the accident, from a Military Justice Auditorate, Master Sergeant Sylvestre. He complains about the lack of cooperation, saying, "I was able to obtain the identities requested only at the cost of a thousand difficulties." He references the Americans in Albertville and grumbles that they don't seem willing to supply any information, and that they are using an excuse that all the proper investigations have been taken care of and all done by them within their own chain of command.

I can fully see that this low-level functionary ran into a few major roadblocks, considering who he was up against. This was a clandestine CIA operation, where personnel were working undercover, and the US government and the CIA were not at all interested in attracting unwanted scrutiny. We had lost an American naval officer and there was every concern that that information should stay confidential. But even taking that into consideration, it never meant that the Agency wasn't going to take care of its own. There was never any doubt or any question about that.

Many of the events of those days are blurry to me now. I don't know if it was a conscious effort to put them aside, or if the years have successfully faded the specifics. But I do know that Roberto Pichardo, Papo Reyes (the Cuban mechanic who had become quite friendly with Gooch), and the rest of the crew that helped prepare the body for transport until the plane could get to us in Albertville all acted out of respect and admiration for a colleague and a friend.

I also know that Dick Johnson had the entire station at the tarmac in Léopoldville, all in appropriate dress, to meet Gooch's body on arrival. After processing, and when the appropriate arrangements were made, a military detail arrived to take his body back to the US.

The Gough family children remember the day well when they heard the news. They arrived home from school and some family friends were there, Frank Kappesser and his wife, Dee. Elonie didn't think anything of it; the Kappessers were frequent visitors. But a priest, Father Alphonse Olive, who was also a family friend, was there as well. He took the children into the bedroom and told them what had happened.

It was a very difficult time for the family. They were not able to get a lot of information from the Agency about the circumstances of Gooch's death. Youngest son Nat was the one who eventually did the research, years later, trying to fit all the pieces together.

Within the last weeks of November 1965 so much had happened. We had successfully run Che Guevara and the communist Cubans out of the country. The government had changed hands as General Mobutu executed a successful coup. "Mad" Mike Hoare's tenure as commander of the Congo mercenary fighting force came to an end. And Gooch lost his life in a precarious encounter with fate.

Marcell Rene Gough, "Gooch" to us, was buried at Arlington National Cemetery on December 6, 1965. He was just forty-one years old.

His son Mickey, who is known as "Little Gooch," remembers that many of his father's UDT and EOD mates were at Arlington that day for the funeral. One of his most vivid memories is of the casket. He describes it as being made of dark, tropical wood. It was a small piece of the Congo that went with Gooch, and then on to his final rest. His name is also inscribed on the memorial wall at the National Navy SEAL Museum in Fort Pierce, Florida, where it belongs.

Chapter Seventeen

True Colors

After we had run Che out of the country and with rebel activity declining, the intensity of our interdiction patrols gradually began to decrease, mostly because of the disintegration of Simba cohesion. The challenge for the mercenary sailors was also reduced because of how our Cuban team had handled the fight alongside the 5 Commando efforts.

It was a lucky thing, because the competence of the mercenary sailors would never rise to the level the professional Cuban sailors brought.

The State Department was never comfortable with the presence of the anti-Castro Cubans in Congo. "Plausible deniability" was barely plausible and the public knowledge of Che and his thugs would only have added to the perception that it was a *quid pro quo*, which certainly was not the case.

From the very day they arrived, the State Department wanted to avoid any political embarrassment that the anti-Castro Cubans' presence might have brought to what was a clandestine effort. The intention was always to have them leave the country as soon as we had adequately trained 5 Commando mercenaries to do the job. So, there was much relief among US government officials when they could use the decreased rebel activity as reason to have my Cuban crew depart Congo quietly, their presence never having been publicly exposed.

By the time of the departure, Chavez and his men had trained the 5 Commando sailors to a satisfactory state of readiness. Our interdiction patrols, the crews' gunfire, and troop-landing support could continue—not as professionally, but at least adequately.

It's difficult for me to overstate their contribution. Brave, competent, determined and totally reliable. They were also a lot of fun to be around. I regretted their departure, but they were never meant to stay and their leaving was always part of the plan. I think because of our unique, challenging circumstances we had forged a mutual trust that was critical for our mission success. And that brought us all close together.

I was also acutely aware that as long as they were in the Congo I had my own small security force that would stand with me against the mercenaries if that ever became necessary. I clearly remember the day they left. The awareness of losing that support and camaraderie started seeping in as I watched them board the WIGMO flight back to Léopoldville, where they would take a commercial flight back to the US. I stood alone on the tarmac kind of holding my breath as the C-46 scrabbled down the runway and caught the air. Alone is definitely alone. And that sensation keeps your head on a swivel. It would be fifty years before I saw any of them again.

Not long after the mercenary sailors had assumed operations, Cassidy came to me and reported that one of the Seacrafts had disappeared. He told me he believed that it had probably sunk. The explanation that it had simply "disappeared" did not seem credible to me.

I made him go over the details several times, telling me everything he knew about the boat's disappearance. But something didn't seem right. My instincts told me that the boat had probably been sold to a buyer on the other side of the lake, maybe in Burundi or Tanzania.. And I suspected that Cassidy was involved in the caper. But of course, there was no concrete proof and any kind of systematic investigation would have been impossible, so I could never be sure of what had actually happened. But I did know this: he was, after all, a mercenary.

At that point, I'm sure he believed that the war was essentially won. In his code of conduct, he had fulfilled his duty and now would be able to leverage his access for his own profit, if possible, from any and all sources. I knew that he would have no compunction otherwise.

When I stated previously that Cassidy was as loyal to me as he was capable of being, this incident is an excellent illustration of that. He would have felt that he met his responsibilities, and from that point on it was "every man for himself," in Cassidy's judgment.

We never heard another word about that "disappeared" boat. Even Tasos's

Greek community network never uncovered any rumors, much less evidence. It's possible that the boat did sink, and I've been judging Cassidy too harshly all these years. But I still believe that it's far more likely that the boat was stolen and sold and then relocated to another of the rift lakes in the region.

I actually felt some relief that it was only one of the smaller PTs and not one of the Swifts. In retrospect, I think it's very possible that if the Cubans had not been present, something like this could have occurred much earlier. Perhaps the entire fleet would have disappeared. I don't know. But maybe if Cassidy and the other mercenaries believed there would be US government retaliation if all the boats disappeared, that would have been helpful, even if it was an unlikely bluff. Because what could one lone ranger do to prevent such theft? That's how I felt there many times, like a lone ranger, faced with duplicity and corruption on both sides, from the mercenaries on our side and the communists on the other.

In reality, there was nothing I could have done if I discovered they had stolen and sold that boat. Except possibly appeal to their perverted sense of duty, if they still retained any. Did they really believe that the US power was behind me? The most potent part of that myth is that it perpetuated my bluff. Because truly, any threat I might have made against them would have been empty, and dangerous, because if they called my bluff, my only recourse was my weapon.

I wasn't the one who paid them; they were on the direct payroll of the Congolese government, so I couldn't withhold their money as punishment. My only way to discipline them was through Cassidy because he was a 5 Commando leader, which I was not. A confrontation with Cassidy would have meant a confrontation with the entire 5 Commando. "One riot, one ranger" is a Texas Ranger phrase known to every Texan. But it would not have been applicable in these circumstances.

All I could do was play along with the "disappeared" story and try to operate the boats in a manner that would make it difficult for any others in the fleet to go missing. I came up with the idea of making Cassidy personally responsible for the safety of the remaining boats, an extension and expression of his sense of "command." It apparently worked, because there were no more suspicious disappearances.

By February 1966, operations had quieted considerably. With our Cuban team having departed and the mercenaries crewing the boats, it was not only less busy but also a whole lot less enjoyable. And the State Department was looking to scale back US involvement considerably.

In a February 16, 1966 memo from Robert Komer to McGeorge Bundy, both from the National Security staff, the question of financing the Congo operations was on the agenda. "Mac," it reads. "[*dollar amount not declassified*] for Congo. I cannot understand why we still have to spend so much to cope with a rebellion that is practically over . . . With your O.K., I had a deal with Helms (then Deputy Director CIA) to review the whole program by March, and see what economies possible. They cut a whole half-million off the air bill—peanuts."

When the 303 Committee met the next day, the issue of funding was front and center according to the minutes of that meeting. The Committee had agreed, when they met the previous October, to conduct reviews of the situation on a quarterly basis, and then to make a consistent effort to cut back wherever and whenever possible. In this February meeting, Bundy lets the Committee members know that by March a plan should be presented with a substantial slash in the budget for the Congo ops.

Larry Devlin was present in the meeting and made the case that even though the rebel activity was down, everyone at the Agency was concerned that they had not been eradicated entirely. He believed a withdrawal of support might jeopardize Mobutu's resolve.

In early March, Secretary of State Dean Rusk sent the embassy in Léopoldville a memo requesting an assessment of the situation, including the effectiveness of the government, prospects for economic stabilization, cohesiveness of the army officers, and an opinion on plans that major opposition forces might increase their influence or assume power.

On March 3, the Chief of the Africa Division for the CIA sent a memo to the Deputy Director of Plans for the Agency requesting that the project in the Congo be formally terminated. The monetary amounts in all of these communications have not been declassified, so getting a feel for the kind of money the US government spent on the war there is difficult. However, the Chief of Africa Division writes that the request for termination is a product of our Navy's success. He writes: "ODACID (State Department) and KUBARK (CIA) believe it is no longer necessary to engage in the large-scale political funding . . . The objectives of promoting stability and moderation remain the same, but the means needed to pursue these objectives are now different."

* * *

In the final days of the Force Navale Congolaise, Cassidy's interest in training Congolese soldiers to take over the Navy began to dwindle. And the quality of the 5 Commando had continued to deteriorate, so Cassidy was adrift.

Although he was never drunk on duty while we were gearing up the Navy and operating the interdiction patrols at a high tempo, I believe that the shrinking of 5 Commando, as contracts ended and the mercenaries drifted off to their respective African countries, fostered Cassidy's inclination to booze and inevitably triggered his paranoia. Cassidy had taken great pride in being a captain in 5 Commando and the senior 5 Commando officer in the Navy, but when it was all coming to an end, I think he felt a huge sense of loss.

There would be no more cowering 5 Commando mercenaries he could intimidate and bend to his will, and little prospect for "liberating" safes and other valuables from the territories occupied by the mercenaries. If he had been involved in the disappearance of our PT, perhaps it was just to try and reconnect with a lifestyle that Cassidy had come to relish. And if he hadn't, then a different conflict would soon provide discipline for him.

The earlier confrontation between Cassidy and Ted Dern had almost ended disastrously with a paranoid and enraged Cassidy wanting to kill Dern in the Palace Hotel bar. Fueled by an over-indulgence in alcohol and Cassidy's hyper-sensitivity with his image, I believe he couldn't think rationally when he thought Dern had disrespected him in front of the men. The only recourse, in his twisted world, was murdering Dern.

As Cassidy's boozing became more frequent and his paranoia more pronounced, it brought him to a lethal confrontation that he couldn't talk out with me and couldn't run away from. His image, his ego, and his hair-trigger temper all contributed to a tragedy when he again felt his power challenged, but this time by a WIGMO contractor.

Cassidy and T. J. Bottomley, a young British aircraft maintenance employee, squared off in a bar. Trevor John Bottomley came out on the short end.

It was late on a Sunday night when Cassidy and a few 5 Commando mercenaries fatefully crossed paths with the WIGMO contractor. The CFL Club, originally a social club for employees of an old rail company, was the scene of the warm-up event.

Bottomley was having drinks with a few friends including another WIGMO employee, Jack Irwin. According to Irwin's account, they heard yelling and screaming coming from another part of the bar. Irwin walked across the barroom and found a South African mercenary named Brian beating the hell out of the club's bartender. When Irwin tried to get him to stop, Cassidy stepped in and told him to keep out of it. As the beating continued, Bottomley then made an attempt to get the mercenary to leave the barman alone. Cassidy turned on Bottomley, telling him that it was a military affair and he'd better stay out of it. Cassidy may have threatened Bottomley, but apparently at that moment, he was unarmed.

The WIGMO contractors left the club and returned to their own bar, the WIGMO "Mess" at the Palace Hotel, arriving there about 11:45 p.m. According to accounts, numerous 5 Commando mercenaries were there that night, including several who were British citizens.

Cassidy and his friends came looking for trouble and entered the WIGMO Mess just after midnight.

As Cassidy walked toward Bottomley, he was slapping a weapon that was now strapped to his side. He glared at Bottomley and said, "I'm not hiding it now."

Trevor Bottomley was evidently fueled by alcoholic hubris that may have gotten him killed. He said to Cassidy. "You're in our mess now, so check your gun at the bar."

Cassidy pulled the 9mm Browning automatic from its holster, cocked it, and pointed it at Bottomley. Demonstrating the perfectly psychotic ire of the mad man he was, pushed the barrel into Bottomley's left nostril and pulled the trigger.

A sickening silence momentarily fell over the bar and no one moved, then chaos erupted. People began ducking for cover and running for the exit. Cassidy turned and pointed the gun at Irwin. "Have you anything to say?" he asked.

Irwin prudently answered, "No, sir."

Cassidy then demanded a drink, and was promptly served by Walter Spencer, the barman on duty that night who would be another eyewitness to give written testimony about the events.

The accounts are buried deep within confidential documents in the British National Archives at Kew, which were sealed until 2001. The now declassified set of papers is filled with communications back and forth between the American and British embassies, the Foreign Office in London, and other consular offices in Zambia, Tanzania, Dar es Salem, South Africa, and Rhodesia (now Zimbabwe). The Interpol representative in Congo was alerted and plans were put in place to send out a bulletin to several African branches, because Cassidy became a man on the run.

The documents reveal that Jim Lassiter entered the bar. He's identified as a US military advisor to the ANC but was actually head of WIGMO AirOps, and therefore a CIA employee. It is reported that without saying a word, Lassiter opened his palm and Cassidy turned over his gun, butt first, into Lassiter's outstretched hand. I'm certain I had never seen Cassidy that willingly compliant.

After the shooting, Lassiter left the bar with Cassidy and took him directly back to his quarters. Cassidy admitted to him that he had gone from the CFL Club to his room, retrieved his weapon, and then to the WIGMO Mess with the intention of killing Bottomley. "It was my hardest killing," Cassidy told Lassiter. "Because I liked the man, I wish I had killed Irwin instead."

The shooting was not initially reported to the local authorities in Albertville because of fear of 5 Commando retaliation if anyone talked or accused Cassidy. I image that his mercenaries were still thoroughly intimidated by the prospect of becoming a victim of Cassidy's paranoia.

With the morning came sobriety, and Cassidy was his cunning self. Last seen about 10:00 a.m., he disappeared at the same moment that two PTs from our fleet went missing. Cassidy and at least two other mercenaries stole the boats and began his escape across Lake Tanganyika. Speculation on his plan was that he would make it to Zambia and from there cross into Rhodesia, where he would have been out of reach of British, Congolese, and American authorities.

But the circumstances in this killing were working against him. Under different conditions Cassidy might have actually pulled off that escape strategy. But he had killed a man who worked for a company with an air force, which put him at a disadvantage. WIGMO planes, piloted by Bottomley's comrades and co-workers, went into the air that day scouring the lake in search of those stolen PTs and hunting for the man who had killed their friend.

These were pilots who were extremely familiar with the Congo terrain. They'd been flying over the area for years and dodging enemy attacks. They knew Lake Tanganyika and they knew what they were looking for. And they had the added incentive of flying a mission on behalf of Bottomley and his brutal murder.

That afternoon, as the pilots soared over the waters of Lake Tanganyika, they spotted the two PTs about fifteen miles from the Tanzanian side. Low on fuel, they returned to base, and two other pilots went up. It was a relentless pursuit to track Cassidy.

Larry Devlin made a trip to Albertville to help find Bottomley's killer. WIGMO was a CIA proprietary; their supply planes were what kept the Agency operable across miles of hard, solid jungle. As station chief, he had a personal interest in the murder of one of their own.

Devlin contacted J. B. Horrocks, vice consul at the British embassy, telling him that Cassidy may be headed to Rhodesia via Zambia, and he suggested that the best way to apprehend him was to alert the Zambian authorities. Devlin had a wide and deep network and this may have been information he received through his sources.

Later in the day, the WIGMO pilots spotted the boats heading south toward Baudouinville, on the Congo side of the lake. Finally, they saw one boat beached a few miles south, and the other boat heading toward the same area. This location was passed to the Zambian authorities. I wonder what may have been going through Cassidy's mind, seeing those planes flying overhead, doggedly pursuing him as he tried to run from the reality of his deed.

The Interpol bulletin and multi-nation advisory was called off two days later when Cassidy was apprehended in Zambia. He had done exactly what Devlin had predicted. The Zambian police took him into custody and delivered him to the Congolese police at the border.

He was sentenced to be executed by firing squad.

Ultimately his sentence was commuted to life imprisonment and he was retained at the Kokolo Military Camp in Kinshasa in January 1967, where he would share a cell with Congolese convicts.

T. J. Bottomley was buried in a Léopoldville cemetery called Kalina with approximately thirty WIGMO friends and colleagues in attendance at the funeral. The British Defence Attaché and Vice Consul Horrocks were also there to pay respects, and the services were presided over by Reverend William Appleby, an English Protestant minister.

George Barnes, the president of WIGMO, flew to England and returned Bottomley's personal effects to his parents in Royston, Hertfordshire.

He was twenty-five years old, just a year younger than I was at the time.

Chapter Eighteen

Mission Complete

With my Cuban crew gone and the missions winding down, it was finally time for me to pack up and leave Congo. I did so exactly as I had arrived: quietly. I boarded that WIGMO C-46 in Albertville with my three pairs of khaki pants, three safari shirts, and a pair of desert boots. Of course, Dick Johnson was at the tarmac to greet me when I arrived in Léopoldville, ever the considerate leader. To my surprise, Dick and his wife and children had kindly arranged a going-away dinner for me, which was to be attended by the entire station.

I almost missed that dinner, however. But only for an exceptionally good reason. I had a rendezvous with Gail, the woman I'd met while convalescing in Léopoldville some months earlier. I hadn't forgotten her.

I had planned an afternoon outing and was able to arrange to take out one of the embassy's eighteen-foot ski boats. We decided to go on a picnic on a sandy beach up the Congo River, which was only the most powerful river in Africa. On average, one million four hundred thousand cubic feet of water flows from the river into the Atlantic every second. It is a wide, and forceful, and unforgiving river. Large pieces of land continually break away throughout the river and are then swept downstream and over Stanley Falls between Léopoldville and the Atlantic Ocean.

These breakaway landmasses are known to be inhabited by snakes and other unfriendly creatures trapped in the tangle of vegetation, so pulling onto a floating island in an emergency would not be a first choice.

We set out on our afternoon adventure and I was fully expecting that we would continue to enjoy the wonderful relationship we had begun when I'd been in Léopoldville the last time. We were powering up the river and I was concentrating on Gail. She was as beautiful as I remembered her and I was having trouble keeping my eyes, and hands, off of her instead of paying proper attention to my surroundings, or even the time of day for that matter. It was really good to see her again.

Then, one of the two outboard motors stopped. I reluctantly shifted my focus away from Gail and pulled up onto one of the floating islands, jumped out of the boat, and tried get the motor running again. I gave it my best shot but couldn't get it started. Snakes, crocodiles, lethal biting insects, none of those hazards came gunning for us, but only because I think we had a lot of luck on our side that day. We climbed back into the boat, determined to make the return trip on one motor.

As I navigated back down the river, attempting to find my way to what passed for a marina back in Léopoldville, I realized a critical error in my captaining. Not having a focus on our surroundings on our ride up the river had been a serious mistake. I was trying, without success, to remember what landmarks we had passed, but they seemed to have changed. There are more than four thousand islands in that river and I think we sailed by all of them.

I tried not to let on to Gail that I was extremely concerned. I had no idea where we were nor how far from the city we'd traveled. I think I pulled off a pretty good act though, reassuring her that she did not need to worry about anything. Maybe it was an even bigger bluff than the one I pulled off with the mercenaries.

I think the Divine Navigator got us back to safety in the end. Just as we made our way to the small dock at the lowly marina, the very last rays of light were falling into a pitch-black sky. I still do not know how it happened. It was pure, blind luck, and as I said, an achievement of Divine navigation.

We made it to the going-away party that Dick and Dell Johnson were throwing for me and acted as if nothing unusual had happened. The party was delightful. Everyone was warm and complimentary and seemed to really enjoy the opportunity for some fun.

We had accomplished something unusual, after all. We had built and trained a mercenary navy, crippled the Soviet-backed Simba Rebel supply lines, thwarted Che Guevara and his thugs, and pulled off a successful covert paramilitary op, possibly the only one of its kind before or since. There was a lot to celebrate. The party was a terrific send off and a satisfying end to a helluva adventure. In the context of the time, we did good.

The next morning, I boarded the plane in Léopoldville and there was Johnson, in his low-key manner, bidding me farewell as he had bid me welcome. My departure was as inauspicious and unnoticed as my arrival. We both knew we had accomplished our mission. But there were no sideboys, no bands, no media, no medals—just an "attaboy" or two, and we all moved on to the next challenge.

I didn't have any further contact with Dick Johnson, ever, which is in keeping with the way compartmenting works in the Agency. One feels those friendships are forever, even though you may never see each other again. I didn't see Larry Devlin again until nearly thirty-five years later, when I interviewed him for this book. He treated me like his long-lost best friend and made me feel most welcomed and appreciated.

Approximately four years after I left the Congo, I was returning to Boston to attend Harvard Business School and I stopped in Athens en route back from Indonesia to the USA. I knew it was a long shot, but I asked a friend of mine who was hosting me and my wife if there was any way he could help me find a Tasos Maillis with a Belgian wife who had been in the Congo. I hadn't had any contact with him over those years so I wasn't even sure he was in Greece.

Our host replied that "Maillis" in Greece was a lot like "Jones" in the USA. But he offered to try, nonetheless, and in less than an hour the phone rang. "Jimmy," a familiar voice resounded. Tasos was only one of a handful of people in my life who ever called me Jimmy. "This is Tasos! Come out to my island to stay."

My wife and I immediately proceeded to the Athens port of Piraeus, where we boarded a ferry to the island of Aegina, as Tasos had instructed. As we came off the ferry, Tasos and his wife Monique were waiting for us. We had a wonderful reunion, and over the next three days, filled with stories told and retold late into the night fueled by homemade moussaka and endless glasses of retsina, we caught up across the intervening years.

Tasos had purchased a small hotel on one of the hills on Piraeus and put us in a room with a glorious view of the Mediterranean.

He explained that life in Albertville deteriorated considerably after the last American departed. Consequently, his focus of activities shifted and eventually he made his way back to Greece. He told me that over the course of that time he had spent a year in England learning about fiberglass. This did not register on me at the moment to be anything of significance. But then Tasos asked, "Have you seen the tourist telephone booths scattered around the city?" I nodded; of course I had, they were everywhere. "Those are fiberglass that I build," he said. "Along with American-style bathrooms." Tasos's enterprising nature had continued to blossom into success.

He then asked me to come down to the dock area with him. "I want to show you something," he said. We left the hotel and walked down to the water toward a fishing dock where Tasos swung open the door of a warehouse. Lying on a boat trailer was the shot-up old hull that I had given him in Albertville five years earlier. Only now, the hull was fully restored to its original condition.

Tasos had shipped the hull back to Greece and used it as his prototype model for the fiberglass boat business he was creating. One of his new business ventures was to sell them as water-ski boats in Greece. I was flabbergasted. He had shipped that damaged hull back from the middle of Africa, attended a fiberglass technical school in England, restored the hull, and made it his production model. That was Tasos's entrepreneurship and creativity to the max.

* * *

After I arrived back in the US, I checked in at Headquarters and moved on to other things. I stayed with the Agency for several years, enjoying my work and getting the opportunity to find out a lot about myself. The work took me to Asia, where I eventually went into business and ended up living for more than thirty years.

My time with the Agency has given me an understanding of what is required of covert operators. People who work at the tip of the spear are sometimes forced to ignore the rules of engagement, which can often become irrelevant in the face of real and imminent threats. Imposed by those with little experience or understanding of the warriors' limited options, they demand hard and fast restrictions on a situation that requires agility of thought and action.

In my opinion, the path to success in covert ops is for our government to develop an officer and NCO corps with such professionalism, integrity, and humanity that rules of engagement are inculcated in their normal behavior.

Then, get out of the way and allow those operators to exercise the common sense and good judgment their training instilled, without fear of unreasonable retribution from the sherry-sippers if anything goes wrong in the chaos of combat.

The Congo adventure is a long way in the background now. But it seems as though little has changed. In 1997, Mobuto was finally overthrown by Laurent Kabila, the very same man who had teamed up with Che and attempted to take power in the '60s. Kabila was subsequently assassinated by one of his own guards in 2001, and his son, Joseph Kabila, took over for his father. He is currently the president of a country where warring rebel factions continue to clash, and is unwilling to honor the results of a recent election and step down from office. Ebola has broken out again and millions of citizens have been plundered, terrorized, raped, and murdered in a seemingly endless conflict in the same area that we had "pacified."

Now, no heroes in the media or Congress want to take up this cause of pacification and rehabilitation of Congo. The photo ops are just not worth the risk. The UN troops are of inconsistent quality and frequently are participants in the continuing rapes and thefts. Plunder of gold and diamonds continues as it always has, with the primary loyalties being to tribes or gangs.

It is easy to say that it was a waste of time, money and lives; that we should have stayed uninvolved; that all we did was exacerbate what had historically been standard behavior. That is intellectually dishonest, because there is no way of knowing how the situation would have turned out if the US government had refrained from involvement. We prevented seizure of the vital resources of Congo by the Soviet bloc and China and, in the process, we did save many lives.

Throughout the documents recently declassified by the US government there are continuing discussions among personnel in all sectors about the future of the Congo. While the US could be accused of an overreaction to a perceived Communist threat and to an exaggerated need to control vital natural resources, which did drive policy to a large degree, other elements are clear when scrutinizing the discussions. Again and again, the US set out goals for the Congo that were humane and generous. The objective was for the country to be stable, financially viable, and not dependent on the US, to have a democratic constitution, and to stand on its own. I feel some pride in having been a part of that.

Chapter Nineteen

Post Script

THE PLAYERS

Sam "Jock" Cassidy

The story of Jock Cassidy didn't end with his "life" imprisonment in a Congolese prison. He secured a release from Camp Kokolo, but the details are as murky as everything associated with events in Congo. The commutation of his "death by firing squad" sentence was somehow due to Cassidy having wrangled an award from the Belgian government, the Order of Leopold, for his services in Congo. This apparently resulted in the death sentence being reduced to life imprisonment. And Cassidy was released from prison altogether. The rumors of his stockpile of gold from the Watsa region must have been true. I'm not sure how he did it or where he kept it, but his final curtain call in the Congo probably depended on that cache of gold to keep him alive and a free man.

The area surrounding Watsa has long been a gold-producing region. Located in the province of Haut-Uele in the northeast near the Uganda border, it has a history fraught with the worst examples of human rights violations and business investment scams inflamed by greed for gold. The series of 5 Commando versus Simba firefights in that region enabled the mercenaries to plunder large amounts of gold. Peters and Cassidy, as senior leaders, were allegedly able to personally grab and stash away a considerable cache.

Cassidy spent only a short time in prison for cold-blooded murder. He left the Congo eventually, and after that I understand he ended up in Johannesburg, South Africa, but from there the trail goes cold. I'm not sure where he spent his next years, nor if he's dead or alive.

John Peters

Peters assumed command of 5 Commando soon after Hoare departed Congo, and eventually achieved the rank of lieutenant colonel. It was assumed that Peters killed or arranged van Oppen's "accidental" firing of his automatic weapon into his own belly, although I believe the actual killing was done by one of his men, ostensibly on behalf of Peters.

I was sitting in the restaurant of the Hyatt Hotel in Singapore sometime in the mid 1970s. I looked across the room and was astonished to see John Peters. It had been more than a decade and a continent away since I'd last seen him, but he was easily recognizable. My reluctance to rekindle a long-dormant relationship with a cutthroat mercenary kept me from going over to say hello. I never ran into him again, but I heard that years later he was killed in Thailand. It was either by the Thai police or a vigilante while he was attempting to fly a quantity of opium out of the country in a C-46.

Mike Hoare

LCol Hoare returned to South Africa and subsequently tarnished his reputation with a comedic attempt at a coup d'état in the Seychelles. His force, disguised as a visiting rugby team, was discovered to be carrying weapons in their rugby bags. They were then forced to flee by commandeering the plane that had delivered them to the Seychelles and they fled to South Africa, where there were legal implications for this silliness.

For a time, Hoare luxuriated in southern France as the proprietor of a bed and breakfast, eventually returning to retire in South Africa, where he has just celebrated his ninety-eighth birthday. He enjoys his well-earned notoriety and the visits from his former troops who romanticize their exploits years earlier in Congo. As Larry Devlin expressed, he was "a gentleman adventurer" who accomplished in the Congo what few others could have equaled.

Marcell Rene "Gooch" Gough

Gooch's presence in the Congo and his contributions to our mission had always been held as classified information and therefore completely unspoken of and without acknowledgment by the government. Until March 2016.

The CIA's memorial wall is located in their original Headquarters building at Langley, Virginia. A white marble commemorative symbol with rows of stars are chiseled into the stone, each representing an Agency employee who died in the line of service. After decades of denial of Gooch's participation as a CIA employee, he finally received what he deserved. With his wife Ida May and his children and grandchildren present, the Agency placed a star on that wall in Gooch's honor.

His son Nat received a personal phone call from then Agency Director John Brennan. Nat says that Brennan wanted to personally express his gratitude for the sacrifice his family made. And Brennan wanted him to know that it was important and meant a lot that the family was coming to Washington for the ceremony.

The Agency finally recognized Gooch's service.

Jordy McKay

McKay went on to a successful intelligence career and is now retired, never adequately or officially recognized for his performance in Congo, but he is held in much esteem by the real operators.

Dick Johnson

Johnson eventually retired after an exemplary career in the Agency. I had no further contact with him after my farewell party at his home in Léopoldville. Helluva fine man.

Tasos Maillis

Over the years, Tasos would get drawn back to Africa, usually to fish or harvest shrimp. We reestablished contact for the last time after he returned to Athens for good. What a man. Tasos died of a stroke a few years ago and not long after Monique passed away. They were quite a team, starting in remote Congo. I was able to visit him to say goodbye, old friend.

Gail

Not long after I departed the Congo, Gail's tour ended. We met in Madrid, which was still under the very conservative influence of General Franco. But that didn't stop us from going out on the town and, of course, dancing. When she got out on the floor wearing a chartreuse outfit, with her auburn hair swinging with the rhythm of the band, her moves were something the locals had not seen performed in years. I was concerned they might call the cops. But they didn't. Maybe because her sexy style was offset by the unwieldy technique of my moves, which must have seemed more like a lurch than a dance step. But we were right back in form, dancing till nearly dawn and soaking in the pleasure of each other's company.

We then proceeded to the Spanish beaches around Torremolinos and spent a few days there in a small Andalucian hotel, listening to flamenco music and hiding out from the rest of the world. We headed out of southern Spain and took a ferry across the Mediterranean to Tangiers. Finally, we ended up in Gibraltar, crossing the border back into Spain on a bus with the locals, including their pigs and chickens.

We parted company in Madrid. Both of our jobs would take us to opposite ends of the world, which made communications difficult to impossible. I heard from her once more, by mail, on my honeymoon in Hawaii, en route to live in Indonesia. So I never responded. Timing is everything. And as the old Frank Sinatra song says, ". . . once in a while, along the way, love's been good to me . . ."

Larry Devlin

Devlin wrote his account of his time in the Congo in his 2007 book *Chief of Station, Congo.* He lived and worked in Africa for several years after leaving the CIA, and passed away in 2008 at his home in Virginia. He was an action-intellectual: WWII combat officer, Harvard, first Chief of Station, Congo. He is the only man I know of who backed down John Peters. The story was told to me by someone who was there. Peters apparently had indiscreetly threatened Devlin, not to his face but openly among the mercenaries. It was probably something along the lines of: "I'm going to kill that son-of-a-bitch when I see him." The details of exactly why Peters was out to get Devlin have been lost. As the story goes, Devlin approached Peters, armed and unflinching. He was, after all, Chief of Station, CIA. "John," he said, "I understand you are looking for me?" Without hesitation Peters replied, "No, Larry, I am not looking for you." How would this story resonate today, over a glass of sherry at a Harvard faculty session?

Bill Hamilton

Bill lived in Virginia Beach, Virginia, for many years, not far from the naval base at Little Creek, the East Coast home of the Navy SEALs that he played a significant role in helping to create. His accomplishments add up to an outstanding career in both the Navy and CIA. He died early 2017 and is buried at Arlington Cemetery. He is survived by his wife Barbara, who still lives in their Virginia Beach home. I wrote a commemoration in the official UDT-SEAL publication, *The Blast*, 1st Quarter, 2017. Hopefully, one day Bill's contributions will receive the recognition he earned.

Lobert Broussard

Broussard still lives in Louisiana near where he first worked for Seward Seacraft, the job that brought him to the Congo. He is beyond age ninety and, at last conversation, still has an excellent memory for the details of his time when he and his fellow Cajuns stitched our boats back together. His original diary and photographs were extremely helpful in telling this story and illustrating our many challenges. Lobert and his crew have never been acknowledged or thanked for what they contributed. Thank you!

THE CUBANS

In efforts to prosecute this war in a clandestine manner, the US relied on these anti-Castro Cuban exiles who were the best available, and who represented operational experience, proven competence, and loyalty. For the US government, they also came with the political convenience of plausible deniability. None of them had US citizenship and many were stateless, having fled Cuba and entering the US without proper paperwork. They were proud professionals, loyal, dedicated, and essential players in the US covert war in the Congo. They are recognized at the new Brigade 2506 Museum and Library in Miami's Little Havana neighborhood.

Ricardo Chavez

Ricardo lives and works in Monterrey, Mexico. He returned to his mother's home country after spending several years in Miami. He is retired and splits his time between Mexico and the US enjoying his eight children and eight grandchildren in Houston, Texas. A most honorable, competent, loyal gentleman.

Roberto Pichardo

Pichardo is active with the Museum of the 2506 Brigade in Miami, the organization that maintains the history of the Bay of Pigs invasion and includes the Makasi pilots and the Cuban Congo Navy, having been one of the participants in all. He is retired and lives in Miami. His son Manny is determined that these men be honored and remembered by posterity and devotes much time and energy to that effort. Pichardo maintains the same spirit he did fifty years ago; a most exemplary man.

Felix Toledo

Felix lives in Miami, and he and his wife Sandra were extremely generous in loaning us their home to conduct interviews. He is retired but works part time as a heavy equipment operator.

Eulogio "Papo" Reyes

Papo, our expert mechanic and engineman, passed away in September 2017. The fact that many of these brave men may not be among us much longer has been a strong motivation to tell this story and to let the world know of their heroism. As we all found out in the Congo, Papo was as good as they get.

Generoso Bringas

Bringas, as everyone refers to him, is retired as well and lives in Miami. He and all these Cuban Congo adventurers have remained good friends throughout the years.

Many of the others of this splendid group are gone now. Their spirits remain in the heart of the Cuban Community and will be kept alive by the determined efforts of sons and daughters like Manny Pichardo and the Museum.

Epilogue

A Reunion Fifty Years Later

In November 2014, an extraordinary reunion took place. On a balmy Sunday afternoon in a suburb of Miami, nearly 250 people came together to honor those who had fought in the Congo. The Makasi pilots and Navy and ground troops were face to face for the first time in fifty years with some of the people whose lives they helped save, who made the pilgrimage to Miami from Europe and Congo.

People flew in from all over the world to meet the men who had risked their lives thousands of miles from home in order to bring innocent victims to safety.

At the time of the crisis in Stanleyville, events transpired quickly and on the fly, and no one had any idea who their rescuers were. As one of the people in attendance at the reunion put it, "We didn't have time to get acquainted." So all these years later, they were finally able to meet and to relive some of their stories. And to say thank you.

Family members who had been taken hostage during the Stanleyville massacre, and who had lost loved ones there, came to the reunion for a chance to identify the faces they'd seen fleetingly as they were hustled out of harm's way and into a waiting C-130 aircraft.

Some of those who were reunited included members of the McMillan family. Five of six McMillan brothers were at the reunion including John, who was thirteen years old at the time. The McMillans, along with seven other missionary families, had been in their compound when the rescue began. The compound was known as Kilometer 8 because of its distance from the center of Stanleyville. The Simbas had been holding everyone there, twenty-five people in all, for the previous four months.

When the Americans, Cubans, and Belgians arrived, their approach was signaled by the sound of heavy aircraft nearby. A BBC broadcast that morning announced that the Americans and Belgians were arriving to rescue hostages. This brought the Simbas, weapons in hand, running toward the compound where the families were being held. John's father, Hector McMillan, and another missionary went outside to speak to them.

One of the Simba Rebels entered the house where the McMillan family lived and began randomly shooting. A bullet got John's older brother Ken McMillan in the hip and another brother, Paul, was grazed on the cheek. Hector McMillan then entered the house attempting to help his family and one of the rebels shot and killed him.

Two hours later several military trucks came rumbling toward them, loaded with well-trained Cuban fighters who shot their way into the compound. John recalls that "They were making so much noise and had so much ammunition and shooting so much" that they had little trouble scaring away any Simbas.

The Cubans loaded the families into their vehicles and transported everyone to the airport to be flown away to safety.

The emergency rush back through town and out to the airfield was filled with defensive gunfire and shouts that the children keep their heads down and their eyes covered. There were a lot of dead bodies in the streets from the atrocities the Simbas were inflicting on the city of Stanleyville. It was a chaotic dash to safety. But the Cubans were calm under fire and the children followed orders.

Once they arrived at the airport, all the hostages were quickly moved out of the trucks and into the planes. There was no time to say goodbye or even thank you. As the planes filled up and traumatized children and families were safely aboard, the Cuban rescuers simply disappeared.

It would be fifty years before these people would see each other again, at this reunion. That afternoon, the thank-yous that had been postponed for half a century occasionally came with a burst of tears.

One odd coincidence in the McMillan family story was revealed at the reunion. In 1964, Bruce Rogers was a twenty-five-year-old US Air Force lieutenant and navigator on one of the C-130s that dropped paratroopers and waited at the airport to fly hostages out. He and John McMillan have both been living in the same very small town of Gig Harbor, Washington, for many years and never knew that they had both been part of the Congo rescue that day, Rogers on the giving end, and McMillan on the receiving end. Even though they both work at the waterfront in downtown Gig Harbor, they had never actually met until the reunion.

Also at the reunion was Richard L. Holm, an extremely well-respected veteran of the Congo operation and a career CIA officer. While in the Congo he was doing recon from the air in a T-28 flown by one of the Makasi Cuban pilots, Juan Peron. A storm blew them off course and they went down, crash landing in a small clearing in the jungle. Holm was doused with aviation fuel as the plane spiraled on the ground. His eyes were singed shut and he was burned over 35 percent of his body.

Peron and Holm got lucky and were befriended by a local tribe who kept Holm alive while Peron went for help. Walking, canoeing, and bicycling nearly 280 kilometers with the help of the tribesmen, Peron found a Belgian outpost. Eventually Holm was flown back to the US by the CIA and treated in the nation's best burn hospital and at Walter Reed. He lost an eye, is severely scarred and has limited use of his hands, but he survived and had a long, successful career at CIA. He and Juan Peron were both at the reunion and have remained lifelong friends.

The reunion was also the opportunity where I was able to see some of my crew members again for the first time in fifty years. This special event came up coincidentally while I was working on this book. Chavez, Pichardo, Toledo, Bringas, and others were there waiting for me when I arrived. We were the representatives of the war fought on the water. It gave me a helluva good feeling to be in their company again. These men were true compadres.

The following is the speech I gave at the event on behalf of the Cuban Congo Navy:

Today we commemorate an event that is evaporating in the mists of time, despite the impact it had on the many children rescued, the subsequent events and further battles in the Congo, and the international repercussions.

We honor the courage and fortitude of these men who were dropped into a very hostile place with a mission to save the lives of the threatened and innocent, with whatever ingenuity and courage they could muster, with minimal prospects for aid if shot or injured. Those who were children at the time of their rescue, and who are here with us today, are the testimony to the results of their rescuers' mighty efforts.

One of the consequences of these events was the creation of a Navy on Lake Tanganyika, to starve the Simba terrorists of weapons and supplies by interdicting the transport across the lake from the terrorist Simba Rebels' support base located at the Port of Kigoma in Tanzania. The second largest freshwater lake in the world, Lake Tanganyika is a massive body of water—450 by 45 miles, a huge funnel capable of six- to eight-foot swells in bad weather. Think about how to patrol that amount of territory, approximately the distance from Miami, Florida to Savannah, Georgia on a fifty-foot platform in the dark, not knowing if, or when, you might encounter hostile fire.

Soon after arrival, we began to receive rumors of Che Guevara and his gang's presence with the Simba terrorists. Needless to say, this was extra motivation for a group of men dedicated to the eradication of communism anywhere and everywhere.

Che's presence indicates to you the support that the Simba terrorists were receiving—including Castro's Cuba, led by Che and his gang, from Eastern Europe, where much of the terrorists' training was being conducted in Bulgaria, from the Soviet Union, and from China, where Premier Chou En Lai was quoted as saying that the key to control of Africa was the Congo. This was the height of Cold War confrontation. Exotic nuclear weapons minerals, some only available from the Congo, were part of the strategic objectives of all parties, communist and non-communist.

These maritime warriors were essentially parachuted into this environment and told to be successful. Except for regular supply flights from the Makasi Air Force, we had no communications with the embassy in Léopoldville (now Kinshasa) except by Morse code and one-time encryption pads. For operational purposes, we were entirely on our own—sixteen Cubans and me. Let me tell you that trust and confidence among this team was essential, as was competence.

In addition to conducting our own patrols, mostly at night, the Cubans were conducting training of the 5 Commando mercenaries, hired and paid by the Congolese government. These men had no experience or expertise with boats and disciplined patrolling. The Cubans had to make these mercenaries into sailors, and quickly, as the US State Department was very nervous about the presence of our Cubans being discovered doing what we were doing.

This training involved two Swifts, on which the Cubans were the world's experts by this time from their raids on Castro's Cuba from bases in Central America, prior to their deployment to the Congo. These two Swifts, in Central America named *Monty* and *Gitana*, were sliced in half, sliced longitudinally, loaded onto C-124 Globemaster airplanes, flown into an airfield on the shore of Lake Tanganyika, moved by narrow-gauged railroad to the Congolese lake port of Albertville, and stitched back together with the assistance and supervision of these Cubans.

The Navy consisted of the Swifts, plus two large vessels commandeered from the commercial fleet, which had previously been employed in Lake commerce. These vessels acted as "mother ships" to six Boston Whaler–type boats. The Swifts could work independently with their own radars, and the Mothership vectored the smaller PTs toward targets identified on the Motherships' radars. Weaponry was captured Russian weapons and a few US big guns.

The interdiction patrols had an immediate effect. Che Guevara admits our impact on his sustainability in his own diary, *The African Dream*. Also, the Navy developed tactics to support the ground units both from offshore gunfire support and with landings along the Congolese coast, where the terrorists had camps to receive the supplies from across the lake.

Before long, this combination of interdiction of weapons and supplies along with increased pressure on the ground produced an outstanding result: defeat of the Simba terrorists, defeat of Che, and defeat of the Communist support effort.

A friend of mine wrote a book some forty years after an intense battle in Central Vietnam that went unnoticed except by those rescued and those who were the rescuers. My friend spent six years and over $100,000 obtaining the recognition for his unit that it had earned and not received, culminating in a Presidential Unit Citation presented by the president in the Rose Garden of the White House.

Here today, we have men of similar courage, who had much less support and attention than did that cavalry unit in Vietnam. And these men, these fine Cuban Americans, will receive no recognition, no medals, no Rose Garden thanks. They have always known that is the way it would be, and they have never asked for more.

What they will have, that no one else can ever deny them, is the respect, admiration, and affection of those few who were there, and truly know how bravely and honorably these men performed; and, of course, the gratitude from those who were saved. What these men had was each other, their mutual trust, respect, their pride in their performance, and their dedication to the eradication of communism.

There were no expressions of entitlement, and there are still none. They took the conditions, circumstances, and threats that were presented, and did what they were tasked with accomplishing. They were not mercenaries. They were paid modestly and did not participate in the looting and theft that was possible, and rampant, in the area. Rather, they were disciplined and proud participants in an historical event saving the lives of thousands, including those we are privileged to have with us today in their desire to salute their rescuers. It is no exaggeration to say that these folks would not have survived that terror without the intervention and performance of these men.

Although I have the honor of speaking on behalf of the Navy, the same courage, ingenuity, pride, and grit was exhibited throughout the entire Cuban-American contingent—the ground force, the air force, and the naval force.

There is one remaining Navy story, however, that I believe that my shipmates will be proud to have revealed to this audience: this Navy, composed of these men and their shipmates who have since passed, in November 1965, engaged in a firefight with Che Guevara and his gang and then chased them across Lake Tanganyika as Che and his gang of thugs fled, surrendering Che and Castro's first attempt to export the revolution. And as Che says in his own diary, the interdiction of his supplies and weapons by this Navy was instrumental in his failure. I believe these men cherish that result, as will all of you in this audience.

Fifty years later, there are lessons in these events relevant to today's war on terror. It takes dedicated men of intelligence, judgment, and courage, willing to go into harm's way to do the job, to protect the lives of the innocent, and to destroy those of perverted political and religious beliefs who seek to harm us.

Please join me and salute these deserving men.

THE END

Bibliography

Baker, Colin
Wild Goose: The Life and Times of Hugh van Oppen
Mpemba Book, 2002, Copyright Colin Baker, 2002

Guevara, Ernesto "Che"
The African Dream: The Diaries of the Revolutionary War in the Congo
Haverhill Press, 2000, Copyright 1999 by *Archivo Personal del Che*

Hoare, Mike
Congo Mercenary
St. Edmunston Press, Paladin edition 2008, Copyright Mike Hoare 2008

Mockler, Anthony
The New Mercenaries: The History of the Hired Soldier from the Congo to the Seychelles
Corgi Book edition, 1986, Copyright Anthony Mockler 1985

Villafaña, Frank
Cold War In The Congo
Routledge; 1st edition, February 17, 2012

US State Department documents—*Foreign Relations of the United States,* 1964–1968 Volume XXIII, Congo, 1960–1968, *Editors:* Nina D. Howland, David C. Humphrey, Harriet D. Schwar, General Editor: Adam M. Howard

The National Archives Documents, (Britain), file FO 1100/53 *Alleged Murder of TJ Bottomley by the British Mercenary Samuel Cassidy*

Endnotes

1. Memorandum from Robert W. Komer of the National Security Council Staff to President Johnson Washington, August 18, 1965. Johnson Library, National Security File, Memos to the President, McGeorge Bundy, Vol. 13. Secret.
2. Telegram from the station in the Congo to the Central Intelligence Agency, Léopoldville, June 13, 1964. Central Intelligence Agency Files, Job 78–00435R, DDO/ISS Files, Box 2, Folder 10.
3. Telegram 1554 from Léopoldville to CIA, October 12, 1965 Fiche 49, Row 2, Frames 6–10.
4. Ibid.
5. Memorandum from Peter Jessup of the National Security Council Staff to the President's Special Assistant for National Security Affairs (Bundy) Washington, May 19, 1964.
6. Ibid.
7. Memorandum for the Record, National Security File, Washington February 8, 1965, Robert W. Komer Johnson Library, National Security File, Country File, Congo, Vol. XI, Memos & Miscellaneous, 1/65–9/65. Secret. Prepared by Komer. Copies were sent to McGeorge Bundy, Fredericks, McIlvaine, and Lang.
8. Memorandum From the Chief of the Africa Division, Directorate of Plans, Central Intelligence Agency (Fields, Glenn D) to the Deputy Director for Plans (Fitzgerald, Desmond) Washington, August 30, 1965. Central Intelligence Agency Files, Job 78–03805R, DDO/IMS Files, Box 3, Folder 11
9. Cryptologic Quarterly, (U) Interlude: Maneuvers and Watchfulness, 3 August, Pg 20 https://www.nsa.gov/news-features/declassified-documents/gulf-of-tonkin/articles/assets/files/release-1/rel1_skunks_bogies.pdf.
10. Memorandum from Robert W. Komer of the National Security Council Staff to the President's Special Assistant for National Security Affairs

(Bundy) Washington, January 26, 1965. Source Johnson Library, National Security File, County File, Congo, Vol. X, Cables, Memos & Miscellaneous, 12/64. Secret.

11. Memorandum from Harold H. Saunders of the National Security Council Staff to President Johnson. Washington, February 25, 1965. Source: Johnson Library, National Security File, Country File, Congo, Vol. SI, Memos & Miscellaneous, 1/65–9/65. Secret.
12. *The African Dream: the Diaries of the Revolutionary War in the Congo,* Che Guevara. Pg 1.
13. Ibid, Pg 184–185.
14. Ibid, Pg 192.
15. Ibid, Pg 192.
16. Ibid, Pg 129.
17. Ibid, Pg 187.
18. Ibid, Pg 193.
19. Ibid, Pg 202.
20. Ibid, Pg 202–203.
21. Ibid, Pg 192.
22. Ibid, Pg 209.
23. Ibid, Pg 210.
24. Ibid, Pg 214.
25. Circular telegram from the Department of State to All African Posts. Source: National Archives, RG 59, Central Files 1964–66, POL 23–9 THE CONGO. Confidential; Priority. Drafted by Canup; cleared by Richard J. Peltier of AF/P, Strong, Root, Ben Thirkield of P, Deputy Assistant Secretary for EUR Walter J. Stoessel Jr., Schaufele, and AFW Director G. Edward Clark; and approved by Trimble. Also sent to Cairo, Brussels, Rome, London, Paris, Bonn, Lisbon, Luanda, and Salisbury.
26. Ibid.
27. Ibid.
28. Telegram from the Department of State to the Embassy in Belgium. Source: National Archives, RG 59, Central Files 1964–66, POL 23–9 THE CONGO. Confidential; Limdis. Drafted by Schaufele; cleared by Brown, Moffat, and Stearns; and approved by Williams. Repeated to Léopoldville and CINCSTRIKE.

29. Congo Mercenary, Mike Hoare, Pg 286.
30. Dispatch from the station in the Congo to the Central Intelligence Agency. Larry Devlin, December 13, 1965 Source: Central Intelligence Agency Files, Job 82-00450R, DDO/AF, AF/DIV Historical Files, Box 6, Folder 6, Leopoldville, 3 Feb 54-Dec 65, [cryptonym not declassified]. Secret; Rybat.
31. Ibid.
32. Memorandum for the 303 Committee. Source: Central Intelligence Agency Files, Job 81–00966R, Box 1, Folder 12, Congo, 1966. Secret; Eyes Only.
33. Ibid.
34. *Congo Mercenary*, Mike Hoare, Pg 14.
35. *The New Mercenaries*, Anthony Mockler, Pg 127.
36. *Wild Goose: the Life and Death of Hugh van Oppen*, Colin Baker, Pg 209.
37. Ibid.
38. "Democratic Republic of Congo: A Study of Binding Constraints," Alfie Ulloa, Felipe Katz & Nicole Kekeh, Pg 6.
39. Ibid Pg 15.
40. *Congo Mercenary*, Mike Hoare, Pg 121.
41. Ibid, Pg 282.

Index

A
Appleby, William, 147
Arroyo, Jorge, 56
Artime, Manuel, 55–56

B
Bain, Bill, 63
Baker, Colin, 125
Ball, George, 106
Barnes, George, 147
Bay of Pigs, 64
Bottomley, T. J., 144–145, 147
Bowens, J. D., 16–17
Bresch, Joe, 63
Bringas, Generoso, 55, 66, 160
Broussard, Lobert, 58–59, 61, 63, 67, 159
Bundy, McGeorge, 13, 35, 106, 142

C
Carney, Daniel, 1
Cassidy, Samuel "Jock," 41–43, 45–47, 72, 81–87, 134, 140–141, 143–146, 155
Castro, Fidel, 20–21, 55, 72, 74–75, 90, 105, 107–109, 118, 165
Cepedo, Serapio, 55
Chavez, Ricardo, 55–57, 64, 71, 73, 76–77, 91–92, 103, 112–114, 118–122, 131–132, 134, 139, 159–160
Cheever, Bruce, 30
China, 21, 105, 153
China Beach, 14
CIA, 4, 24, 30–35, 56, 67, 69, 92–93, 106, 117, 142–143, 156–157
Clines, Tom, 20–21, 36, 55, 57–58, 64–65
Close, Glenn, 102
Close, William, 102
Congo
  Simba Rebels in, 19–23, 36, 90
Cosme, Luis, 65
Cuba, 20–21, 27, 36, 55–57, 64–66, 70–77, 90, 93, 105–106, 108–109, 165
Cuban Missile Crisis, 65, 89

D
Dengue fever, 101–102
Dern, Ted, 78–79, 81, 83–87, 131, 143
Devlin, Larry, 26, 35, 43, 117, 125, 142, 146, 151, 156, 158

E
Ebola, 102
Ermans, 22–24, 53, 74, 76, 89

F
Fernandez Mell, Oscar, 108–109
Force Navale Congolaise, 21, 26–27, 41, 51, 60, 94, 101, 120, 143
Frogmen, 5–6

G
Gattis, Phil, 30
Gibby, Curt, 29
Gitana, 55–56, 59, 63, 66, 68, 76
Godley, G. McMurtrie, 35–36
Gough, Rene, 69–71, 74–75, 78–79, 85, 134–135, 137, 156–157
Guevara, Che, 20, 27, 90, 93–94, 103–105, 107–109, 111–113, 118, 137, 139, 150, 164, 166

H
Hamilton, Bill, 20–21, 30, 36, 54–55, 57–59, 61, 63, 66, 69–70, 159
Harriman, Averell, 106
Hidalgo, Ken, 59
Hoare, "Mad" Mike, 1, 22–26, 38, 43–45, 78, 104, 116–117, 123–125, 136, 156
Holm, Richard L., 163
Horrocks, J. B., 146–147
Huston, John, 59

I
Irwin, Jack, 144–145

J
Jessup, Peter, 53
Johnson, Dick, 33–35, 38, 41, 52, 66, 99–101, 137, 149–151, 157
Johnson, Lyndon, 15, 78
Johnson Dick, 33

K
Kabila, Joseph, 153
Kabila, Laurent, 90, 108, 153
Kennedy, John F., 16, 35, 65
Kenya, 23
Kivu, 45
Komer, Robert W., 19, 142

L
Lassiter, Jim, 145

M
Maillis, Tasos, 50–53, 121, 140–141, 151–152, 157
Makasi Cubans, 98, 106–107, 113
McCone, John A., 69
McKay, Jordy, 19–27, 92, 104, 136, 157
McMillan, Hector, 162
McMillan, John, 162–163
McMillan, Ken, 162
McMillan, Paul, 162
McNamara, Robert, 10
Mobutu Sese Seko, 101, 115–117, 128, 153
Mockler, Anthony, 125
Monty, 55–56, 59, 63, 66, 68, 73, 76
Movimiento Recuperación Revolucionaria (Revolutionary Recovery Movement) (MRR), 55, 57
Mundandi, Joseph, 108–109
Munson, Jim, 13–14

N
Nendaka, Victor, 127
Nicaragua, 55
NSA, 93
Nuclear weapons, 89–90

P
Patterson, Ray, 5
Peron, Juan, 163
Peters, John, 43, 123–126, 155–156, 158
Peterson, Bob "Pete," 16
P. G. Thulin, 57
Pichardo, Roberto, 55–56, 64–65, 68, 70, 74–76, 126–127, 131–132, 134–135, 137, 160
Puta, Georges, 137

R
Reyes, Eulogio "Papo," 55, 66, 134, 137, 160
Rhodesia, 23, 72, 146
Rogers, Bruce, 162
Rogers, Robert, 24
Roques, Jacques, 114
Rusk, Dean, 14, 115–116, 142
Rwanda, 108–109

S
Sewart, Fred, 54–55, 59
Sierra Aránzazu, 56
Sierra Maestra, 56
Simba Rebels, 19–23, 36, 90, 101, 129, 150, 162

South Africa, 23, 72
Southern Methodist University, 5
Spencer, Walter, 145

T
Tanzania, 21, 92, 107–108, 111, 114–115, 118, 120
Tarbox, Tom, 10
Toledo, Felix, 71, 77, 91, 93, 113–114, 119–120, 160
Tshombe, Moise, 44

U
Urundi, 22–24
USS *Maddox,* 15
USS *Maryland,* 6
USS *Turner Joy,* 15
USS *Vega,* 5–6

V
van Oppen, Hugh, 124–126, 156
Van Wyk, Johannes, 134
Vietnam, 11, 13–17, 30–32, 64
Villafaña, Frank, 106
Von Lieres Und Wilkau, Hans, 134, 136

W
Widmark, Richard, 5
Wild Geese, The (Carney), 1
Wilson, Edwin, 56

Z
Zambia, 146